What people are saying about *Humanizing Outdoor and Environmental Education* and *201 Nature and Human Nature Activities* by Clifford E. Knapp and Joel Goodman

"Edited by leaders in the field, this is a deeply felt and compelling compendium of some of the forward thinking about the new nature movement and its potential to move our culture forward, not back, to nature."

Richard Louv
Author of Last Child in the Woods, The Nature Principle, and Vitamin N

Joel and Cliff's lifetime work has touched the lives of millions of people. I am delighted that their two new books will continue to make a meaningful, mindful, and heartfelt difference on the planet. These two books are ideal for YMCAs, camps, schools, families, and other settings where we can reach and teach young people and the young at heart about the gifts and blessings of nature and human nature. These books are filled with hundreds of inspiring, intriguing, interesting, insightful, innovative, impactful invitations and activities to help honor Mother Nature and the human spirit at the same time.

Rev. Bruce Tamlyn
Chaplain and Director of Spiritual Life, Silver Bay YMCA

When I first met Joel and Cliff 50 years ago, they were on the ground floor of getting their profound and utterly wise ideas about Environmental Education into the hands of teachers. I was lucky enough to have those two young geniuses as students when I was doing my pioneering work in Values Clarification. I'm so proud to see the gift they have written for you.

Sidney B. Simon, Ed.D.
Professor Emeritus, University of Massachusetts, Amherst
Co-author of Values and Teaching and Values Clarification: A Handbook of Practical Strategies for Teachers and Students

Cliff Knapp's and Joel Goodman's values, vision, passion and working knowledge of nature and human nature are exemplified in these books. Their warm, empathic beliefs in a sense of community and a sense of wonder in the natural world come through clearly. I wholeheartedly recommend these books to you!

Gordon Kaplan
Executive Director (1996 - 2016) American Camp Association, Illinois

"*Humanizing Outdoor and Environmental Education* and *201 Nature and Human Nature Activities* are full of great ideas, examples and reflections on how youth leaders can build appreciation and knowledge of the natural world while at the same time develop self-awareness and interpersonal skills in their participants. This is a gift that young people growing up in the digital age need now more than ever in order to learn the joy and value of balancing screen time indoors with sensory time outdoors."

Donna Ducharme
Chairman, Franklin Grove Creek and Preservation Corporation

As a staff member of a camp based on the writings of Cliff and Joel, I have witnessed the positive impact that this book has had on countless youth from around the country. The abundance of field-tested and classroom-tested activities in these pages has truly enriched so many lives. Joel and Cliff inspire us to treat nature with care and respect and to live with each other in this way as well.

Alan Bartenhagen
Staff, Human Relations Youth Adventure Camp

In this delightful pair of books, Joel and Cliff show that learning is natural: nature has a lot to teach all of us. These two books provide a banquet of thought-provoking insights about the connection between nature and human nature. They are filled with practical, positive, participatory, playful, powerful activities that will engage and enrich the lives of students, campers, adults, and everyone with an interest in living a life connected to the natural world.

Dr. Matt Weinstein
Founder and Emperor of Playfair, Inc.
Co-author of Playfair: Everybody's Guide to Noncompetitive Play

We talk about the growing importance of connecting with nature and connecting with each other. Few books will give you so many wise and wonderful ways of turning this wishful thinking into concrete action – the kinds of action which ensure that however much we upgrade our digital connectivity we do not downgrade our connection with, and enjoyment of, the human and natural world.

Dr. Roger Greenaway
Reviewing Skills Training
Stirling, Scotland

Cliff Knapp and Joel Goodman's two guides blend theory and practice in useful ways. Several chapters provide teachers and group leaders with a rich set of activities to enhance nature awareness and make meaning out of learning experiences. Other chapters present the thinking behind such activities from people like Richard Louv, Cheryl Charles, Joseph Cornell, and Roger Greenaway who have devoted their careers to finding ways to enhance people's connection to the natural world. I will make regular use of these volumes as I plan my own retreats and workshops.

Dr. Gregory Smith
Co-editor/co-author of Ecological Education in Action, Place-Based Education in the Global Age, and Place- and Community-Based Education in Schools

As a former Boy Scout, it's so refreshing to see books that humanize the environment. I mean, that's what we all are—humans in the environment. Joel Goodman and Cliff Knapp have put together a wonderful resource that puts joy and respect into learning about nature. These two books should be part of every young person's education.

Ron Culberson, MSW, CSP, CPAE
Speaker, Humorist, and Author of Do it Well, Make it Fun
Past President, National Speakers Association

As a child participating in Cliff and Joel's programs and later as a young adult staffing them, their educational approach and outdoor activities played a formative role in my personal growth. As an adult working in the field of outdoor education, leading teen wilderness programs and church youth groups, their work mentored my professional development and I applied it to people of all ages and abilities. Any outdoor educator or wilderness guide who needs to expand their range of offerings would serve their clients well by using these books as a guide. Any parents who wish to promote a vital connection to the natural world for their children should carry copies on their family adventures. I am confident that these two books will become as tattered, dog-eared and coffee-stained as mine.

John Friauf, LCSW-R
Outdoor Educator, Licensed Guide, School Social Worker

As our world grows more high tech and as the pace of our lives becomes faster, the need to connect with the natural world and ourselves grows critical. It has become important for educators to find ways to integrate nature and human nature into their curriculum plans. The combination of community building, values clarification, and outdoor adventure is essential and compelling. When you use the ideas in these books, you will witness an amazing transformation of your participants, your staff and even yourself!

> *Wanda DeWaard*
> *Outdoor Educator and Program Consultant, Earth Kin Programs*

Cliff Knapp and Joel Goodman have revised and expanded on the first edition of this valuable experiential learning book. Their work has always been focused on bridging human and natural communities, with special attention to the experience of the learner as an individual and as part of the group. *Humanizing Environmental Education* and *201 Nature and Human Nature Activities* offer educators two timely guides for thinking about and planning authentic experiences that inspire deep learning and commitment.

> *Dr. David Greenwood*
> *Associate Professor and Canada Research Chair*
> *Department of Environmental Education, Lakehead University, Thunder Bay, Ontario*

At a time in history when meaningful personal interaction is overpowered by social media, multi-tasking and an obsession with time-saving, it's refreshing to find a book that celebrates the individual and gently presses us to consider ways to humanize learning. *Humanizing Outdoor and Environmental Education* and its companion *201 Nature and Human Nature Activities* are welcome additions to a societal landscape that often fails to balance content concerns with substantive concern about the well-being of the learner. Thanks to Cliff Knapp and Joel Goodman, we have a tool to restore that balance.

> *Dr. Herb Broda, Professor Emeritus, Ashland University*
> *Author of Schoolyard-Enhanced Learning and Moving the Classroom Outdoors*

For many years I have consulted this guide for inspiration, validation, and important ideas for connecting humans to nature. I know of no other guide that is so easy to use, packed with easily digestible ideas, and stories for bringing humans into the nature equation. When some people focus on the environment, they leave out humans! Big mistake! I am happy to endorse these books and am excited to see the updated versions.

> *David Stokes*
> *Naturalist, Educator, Entertainer*

These books are filled with ideas that guide participants to a holistic understanding of love of others and love of the Earth. The authors recommend that those who teach about the Earth can benefit from those who teach about People. We must strive to truly love one another AND to love the Earth and these books will help create a better world.

> *Thomas E. Smith, Ph.D.*
> *Clinical Psychologist, Outdoor Therapist, Personal Growth Facilitator*

It is time to revive the excitement and creativity of experiential outdoor education! We have widely come to realize the costs of what Richard Louv has called "nature-deficit disorder." Now, more than ever, we as teachers, parents, grandparents, outdoor education staff, and park personnel need to engage our students, children, and park visitors in the kind of experiences in nature that these wonderful books invite us to explore. Ground yourselves in the ideas, principles, and activity ideas these handbooks provide, and get outdoors, in good company, for the joy of it.

> *Barbara L. Glaser, Ed.D.*
> *Co-Founder, Great Camp Sagamore and Sagamore Institute of the Adirondacks*
> *Regional Commissioner, New York State Dept. of Parks*

We suffer because our inaccurate stories separate us from the attractive balance and beauty of Nature in and around us. Happily, *Humanizing Outdoor and Environmental Education* and *201 Nature and Human Nature Activities* provide stories and activities that invite children to visit natural areas where authentic Nature helps them relate with human nature.

Michael J. Cohen, Ph.D.
Director, Project NatureConnect

The survival of civilization depends on the development of an environmental ethic and of behaviors supporting that ethic and a growing concern for a more humanized society. It is imperative that we increase environmental awareness in order to save and protect our planet, our one world. These books show us not just what to do to be connected with our natural world but how to do it while maintaining connections with each other. The character-building, "ageless" activities in these books can be used at home, in the classroom, at nature centers, at camps, adult retreats, and for celebrations of all kinds to gracefully merge both nature awareness and human nature.

Beverly Lazar Davis, LCSW-R
Founder, Youth²: Youth Helping Youth
Licensed Clinical Social Worker
Past Supervisor, Youth & Family Services Team

The Rev. Dr. William Sloan Coffin had a way with words: "The world is too dangerous for anything but truth and too small for anything but love." Having led church youth groups for 40 years, the truth is I love these books. This dynamic duo of books will be especially valuable for adult educators, church youth group advisors, and environmental activists. Joel and Cliff have developed a potpourri of practical, step-by-step learning activities leading to an appreciation of nature and the unique gifts every human being has.

Rev. Jay Ekman
Retired Pastor, Presbyterian-New England Congregational Church

These two books are a beautiful blend of the powerful philosophy and practice of humanizing experiential education. The books are loaded with stimulating invitations for people to engage in active and interactive learning. As a coach, I was particularly intrigued and inspired by the grand slam home run chapter on "Creative Leadership: A Humanistic Approach to Coaching"—that was worth the price of admission by itself.

Brian Hamm
Amherst College Baseball Head Coach
Winningest Coach in 157 Years

An understanding of our human relationship to nature has never been more needed than it is today. In native cultures we speak of seven generations, the understanding that what we do now will impact all who follow us for many years to come. Those who will benefit the most from the important teachings in these beautifully written and carefully thought-out books are our children—the ones who truly are the hope for seven generations and more, for a future that extends far beyond fiscal years or presidencies.

Joseph Bruchac, Ph.D.
Author of more than 120 books including Keepers of the Earth: Native American Stories and Environmental Activities for Children

Joel Goodman and Clifford Knapp are legends in the world of environmental education. Their 1981 book, *Humanizing Environmental Education* is a classic in the field and helped to propel a movement. It is exciting to know that they are again sharing their wisdom and inspiration.

Jane Sanborn and Elizabeth Rundle
Co-authors of 101 Nature Activities for Kids

HUMANIZING OUTDOOR AND ENVIRONMENTAL EDUCATION

A
THOUGHT-FULL
GUIDE FOR
LEADING NATURE
AND HUMAN
NATURE ACTIVITIES

Clifford E. Knapp
Joel Goodman

ISBN: 978-1-60679-384-8
Book layout: Cheery Sugabo
Cover design: Cheery Sugabo
Cover photo: Sagadogo/iStock/Thinkstock
Back cover author photos: Ed Puletz (Clifford E. Knapp); Saratoga Photographer (Joel Goodman)

Healthy Learning
P.O. Box 1828
Monterey, CA 93942
www.healthylearning.com

DEDICATION

This book is dedicated to the people of the communities of which I have been a part—family, school, camp, religious, therapeutic, and other human communities, where I have touched and been touched. I am especially indebted to Nancy Churchill for her emotional and technical support. There have been so many others in my life who have supported me personally and professionally that space does not permit me to list them here. You know who you are! I am blessed.

—C.E.K.

To Jeff McKay, who is a living model of someone who has creatively blended caring for people and caring for our environment. To Matt Weinstein, who practices what he teaches as the Master of Playfulness. To Sylvia Cowan, whose ethics and actions to make this world a better place are inspirations to me. To Jim Edler, whose commitment to combating oppression and racism is an incredible model. To Taffy Colker, whose good heart has traveled the world and written about it so eloquently. I truly cherish them and their friendship, support, innovative thinking, and pioneering spirit as wonderful gifts. I am blessed that each of them has been a dear friend and colleague for almost 50 years. Of course, my wife, best friend, and colleague for 44 years, Margie Ingram, has been an incredible wife and book midwife as Cliff and I gave birth to twins—*Humanizing Outdoor and Environmental Education* and *201 Nature and Human Nature Activities.*

—J.G.

Humanizing Outdoor and Environmental Education

FOREWORD I:
JACK CANFIELD

When I was a kid, I was a boy scout, went to summer camp, and went on family outings with my brothers and sister and parents. I learned to build a fire without matches, to recognize about fifteen bird calls, to swim across a lake, to row a boat, and to paddle a canoe. Along with my mother I helped nurse birds with broken wings back to health. In the summer I would climb the hills behind our houses in Ohio and West Virginia and hunt for snakes and rabbits. In the winter I would climb to the top of a nearby hill to look for deer or to feed the squirrels that were always there. Nature and the outdoors were very much a part of my life. I felt a kinship with all nature and all forms of life.

The beauty of this book, which Joel Goodman and Cliff Knapp have created, is that it helps us all to reclaim the boundless life that lies dormant within us and so dangerously threatened around us. The book artfully weaves together activities that expand our consciousness of ourselves and of the natural world around us at the same time. The worlds are not as different as they would appear at first glance. Every time I learn to love myself a little bit more, I find that I love all of life a little bit more. Every time I come to a new understanding of the natural processes that abound all around me, I come to more fully understand the natural processes of growth and change that exist within me. The principles are the same—cycles, growth, maturation, decay, rebirth, cooperation, competition, assimilation, integration, and so on. We are of a whole. Whatever affects me affects that which is about me and vice versa.

I have been a classroom teacher, a teacher of teachers, a camp counselor, and a transformational trainer. I found that as a professional aid, this book is more than a gold mine of ideas, new perspectives, and practical methods. It is really six or seven books disguised as one. The book contains more activities than you could ever use in two years of teaching or in a lifetime of camp experiences. I am both amazed and impressed at the depth and breadth of what Joel and Cliff know and share with us in this book.

Whether you are a teacher, camp counselor, wilderness trip facilitator, scout leader, environmental educator, concerned parent, or simply a seeker of the wonder and beauty of the universe and the "youniverse," you are lucky to be reading these words, because as soon as you turn a few more pages, you will have embarked upon a great adventure of healing and wholling yourself and the planet. Have a great trip and enjoy sharing it with others.

—Jack Canfield
Co-creator, #1 *New York Times* best-selling series *Chicken Soup for the Soul®*
Author, *The Success Principles: How to Get From Where You Are to Where You Want to Be*™
www.jackcanfield.com

FOREWORD II:
JOSEPH CORNELL

Dr. Joel Goodman and Dr. Clifford Knapp give us a warm and sensitive approach to environmental learning. Our personal emotions and attitudes powerfully influence the way we view nature, and this is why the really good educator nurtures a sense of well-being in the child. It's as important to get the child to feel good about (and in) nature, as it is to inform him of issues in conservation and ecology.

The authors have been involved in camp and school programs where respect for self and others, trust and caring, cooperation, and a sense of community are explored. Dr. Knapp has described his "secret formula" for these programs like this: "First, I invite the best people I know to join our staff; then campers or students come who want to share outdoor adventure and also to improve their relationships with people. The last step is to give a great deal of energy to helping the group work and play as a community. Fun, learning, and caring just don't appear magically in our lives."

This book shows how Joel Goodman and Cliff Knapp make it work. It will tell you how to teach and encourage: interpersonal rapport, open-mindedness, and curiosity; a sense of values (personal, social, and environmental); feelings of self-worth and confidence; and a community spirit among children and adults alike.

I met Cliff Knapp several times over the years and was impressed by his gentle and sincere nature. I feel that he is an effective communicator for a loving and caring approach to outdoor and environmental education. He and Joel Goodman have written a book that truly "covers all the bases" in humanizing the field. It is thorough, useful, and always puts the child's highest good—body, mind, and soul—first. I feel that the book will play an important role in helping us to lovingly encourage the child's awareness of and enthusiasm for nature and human nature.

—Joseph Cornell
Founder and President, Sharing Nature Worldwide
Nature Awareness Educator and Author

Humanizing Outdoor and Environmental Education

CONTENTS

COMING TO TERMS WITH THE TRIP

Throughout our two companion books (*Humanizing Outdoor and Environmental Education* and *201 Nature and Human Nature Activities*), the masculine shall be deemed to include the feminine and vice versa.

There are several terms used throughout the two books that need further explanation. In describing students in a classroom, campers, members of a family, people in an organization, and athletes on a team, we use the word "participants." In speaking of teachers, naturalists, camp leaders and counselors, parents, coaches, and other helping professionals who might use the activity ideas in this book, we use the word "staff" or "leader." In talking about planned and structured activities for a classroom, nature center, outdoor school, camp, family, recreation center, and other arenas in which outdoor and environmental education could take place, we use the word "program" or "curriculum." As you read this book, please make your own personal translations when you come across any of these words.

As you'll see, we have presented a wealth of strategies that invite active participation and learning in these two books. In some activities, the directions are given to the staff. In other activities, they are stated as if given directly to the participants. In all activities, our first mantra is "Safety first!" With awareness of your group's abilities and limitations, we encourage you to use your creativity and good judgment in implementing or adapting the activities to maximize both safety and learning.

CHAPTER 1
WELCOME TO THIS BOOK

"A child cannot reach self-actualization until his needs for security, belongingness, dignity, love, respect, and esteem are all satisfied."

—Abraham Maslow

It was seven o'clock in the morning, and the counselors had just awakened the campers. Everyone, except Harold, got up quickly and prepared for a typical day at camp. Harold was tired, and he pulled the sleeping bag up over his head. After about 15 minutes more of hiding and groaning, Harold decided to get up. He slowly reached underneath his bunk, found his IALAC sign, and pinned it on his pajamas. He was tired because he stayed up late for astronomy the night before.

"Get up, lazy. Let's get with it, or you'll be late for breakfast," shouted his counselor. (Rip! Part of his IALAC sign was torn away with that remark.) Harold quickly threw on his clothes and looked around for his shoes. Apparently someone had hidden every pair he owned. (Rip! More of his sign disappeared.)

He looked around desperately for someone to help him search, but everyone else had gone to the dining hall. He searched everywhere, but he could not find his shoes. When he went into the bathroom to look, he spotted what someone had scribbled on the mirror with soap. It said, "Harold has sleeping sickness." (Rip! More of his sign was shredded.)

He found someone's "flip-flops" in the shower and hurriedly slipped them on. When he arrived at breakfast late, one table of boys stood up and pointed to him and laughed at him. (Rip!)

When the camp director noticed Harold's footwear, he said firmly with a scowl, "You know the rules, get back to your cabin and put some shoes on." (Rip!)

Harold went back to his cabin and finally found his shoes in somebody's locker. He returned to the dining hall, just in time to see the cook close the serving window. He knew the cook saw him, but the window was closed anyway. (Rip!)

"Oh well," Harold thought, "It's not the first time I've gone without breakfast."

His first activity that morning was softball and he really was looking forward to that. Two captains who picked the best players first formed the teams. When the teams were even, Harold was the only one left unpicked. The captains had picked both girls and boys whom Harold knew couldn't even hit the ball. "You take Harold," scoffed one captain.

"No, you take him," said the other, "We want to win today." (Rip!)

At lunch, Harold was squeezing between two tables with a loaded tray when someone stuck out a foot. All Harold could hear after the tray of food came to rest was the word "clumsy," and laughter and applause in the background. (Rip!)

He couldn't hear the other words being said, because the laughter and applause were too loud. (By now you may have figured out the letters in the IALAC sign stand for "I Am Lovable and Capable." Each time Harold was put down and his sign was torn, he felt less confident and good about himself.)

Humanizing Outdoor and Environmental Education

Harold thought the nature class would go better, because he liked the counselor. Everything went smoothly, until someone found a garter snake on the trail. Harold never did like snakes, and it showed. The girl who found it thrust it into Harold's hands, and as he jumped in horror, he tripped over a log behind him. "Nice slide; you're safe at home," the girl said. (Rip!)

Everyone giggled. (Rip!)

The counselor picked Harold up and said with a smile, "My little sister's not even afraid of garter snakes, and she's four years old." (Rip!)

That night, when Harold sat on the edge of the bed to remove his tattered IALAC sign, he hoped that tomorrow would be easier to get through. He did not feel very lovable and capable today, and he hoped that, somehow overnight, his sign would regain some of the lost pieces. How could Harold's day have been better?

The people around Harold could have behaved very differently. His counselor could have said, "It's hard getting up, when you get to bed late. How was astronomy?"

Some campers did not have to hide Harold's shoes.

The soap scribble on the mirror could have read, "Good morning, Harold. Please hurry to breakfast. We want you to sit with us."

Someone at the table could have said, "I'm glad you made it; I saved you a peach."

The director could have said, "Those 'flip-flops' will never get you up a mountain today. I care about your feet, so please put shoes on after breakfast."

The cook could have held the serving window open and said, "There's always room for one more. I think you'll like breakfast today."

One captain could have said, "I'm picking Harold first today, because he's my friend."

Instead of laughing and applauding with two hands, someone could have reached down with one hand and helped Harold up when he tripped.

There could have been so many ways that the people around Harold could have added pieces to his IALAC sign and not torn them away.

This book is written for the teachers, camp leaders, naturalists, parents, and other adults who have opportunities to enrich the life of Harold and other young people like him. What you do with the IALAC idea is up to you.

Since this is a thoughtful guide to leading nature and human nature activities, we will start by exploring how you can get the most out of your journey through the pages of this book. Every guidebook needs descriptions of some of the places you will want to visit, as well as a list of what to take.

Guidebooks are useless unless you know where you are going. The following are some ideas to help you determine which routes you would like to follow. Make a note of the questions that you would like answered:

❑ What does this book have to offer me? What does the term "humanizing outdoor and environmental education" mean? (See Chapter 1—"Welcome to This Book.")

❑ What are some possible goals and organizing principles for humanizing and environmentalizing my program or curriculum? (See Chapter 2—"Designing Your Program or Curriculum.")

❑ What is the "New Nature Movement" and what is happening in the United States and abroad to support this trend? (See Chapter 3—"Two Views of the New Nature Movement.")

❑ What does a seasoned naturalist believe about how to connect people and nature? (See Chapter 4—"Traveling the World, Bearing Nature's Gift of Peace.")

❑ What does the life-skills approach to outdoor and environmental education look like in practice? How can adventure activities in the outdoors be used as a vehicle to promote personal learning and professional development? (See Chapter 5—"Adventure Learning: Personal and Group Challenges.")

❑ How can I become a better facilitator of the learning process so that the participants gain more meaning from the experiences I lead? (See Chapter 6—"Looking Back and Looking Again: Reflecting and Reviewing.")

❑ What are some of the principles underlying a noncompetitive approach to playing? How can I build cooperation, inclusion, and self-esteem through play and recreation? (See Chapter 7—"Playfair: Everybody's Guide to Noncompetitive Games.")

❑ What are some guidelines and specific suggestions for humanizing athletics and other traditional forms of outdoor activity? How can I mix the following ingredients: challenge, cooperation, individual excellence, joy, and learning? (See Chapter 8—"Creative Leadership: A Humanistic Approach to Coaching.")

❑ How can I put all the pieces together into an outdoor program? How has a youth camp incorporated awareness, community building, communicating, valuing, self-esteem, adventure learning, noncompetitive play, and humanistic athletics? (See Chapter 9—"Human Relations Youth Adventure Camp: A Model That Really Works.")

❑ What are some kernels of wisdom that could inspire, challenge, and motivate me? (See Chapter 10—"Can I Quote You on That?: Quenching Quest for Quintessential Quotable Quotations")

❑ Where do I go from here? What resources can provide me with follow-up help? (See Chapter 11—"Resources: Where Do You Go From Here?")

If you are looking for even more, the following is an "extra credit" idea for you to consider: This book has a delightful companion book, *201 Nature and Human Nature Activities*. In our companion book, you will find a gold mine of practical, powerful, enjoyable, experiential activities for people of all ages. These activities will help you put into practice the thought-full philosophy of the book you are now holding. Refer to the Resources chapter for more on *201 Nature and Human Nature Activities*.

This dynamic duo of books will help to answer a variety of questions, including the following:

❑ As a parent, how can I help my children appreciate themselves, their friends, and the environment?

❑ As a teacher, how can I enrich my curriculum and instruction with hands-on, easy-to-implement, learning activities?

❑ As a camp director, what new ideas, approaches, and activities can I use with staff and campers to make our program more exciting, inviting, and effective?

❑ As a camp counselor, how can I supplement my activity skills (e.g., archery, crafts, geology, waterfront) with human relations skills?

❑ When working with youth groups, how can I help young people practice the skills they will need for the rest of their lives, such as communicating, listening, decision-making, resolving conflicts, and empathizing?

❑ As an environmentalist, how can I help people see themselves as *part of* nature rather than separate from it?

❑ In my work in coaching and recreation, what games can be played that give enjoyment and insights about how to play the larger game of life in healthier ways?

Which questions stimulated your curiosity and made a connection with your personal or professional life? These are your clues for finding the treasures buried between the four covers of this book and its companion book. We encourage you to plan your own personalized treasure hunt. In planning your journey, you might want to consider the following things to take:

❑ *Curiosity and open-mindedness:* These books contain hundreds of new ideas for you to ponder. For each usable idea you discover, try to think of at least one way to use it.

❑ *Creativity:* The power of programs and curriculum will increase dramatically if you are willing to modify and adapt these ideas and make them your own. We encourage you to create at least one new way to adapt what we have provided as "food for thought."

❑ *Risk-taking and enthusiasm:* Your willingness to actually try out these new ideas is what will ultimately make the difference. We support you in your efforts to take the ideas from these pages and put them into practice.

❑ *A target:* The ideas in these books are best used when they are targeted upon your goals, principles, and objectives. This factor implies that your actions will only "work" if they are appropriate to the readiness level and needs of the group with whom you are working (or playing). The program and curriculum ideas are not "magic"—you must provide some magic in fitting them to the right situation and group.

❑ *Support:* As in any new venture (or adventure), we often benefit and have more fun with the resources and support of others. We recommend that you consider establishing a formal or informal support group of friends, colleagues, and/or staff members as you think of ways to use these ideas. Discussing the content, adapting it to your situation, and thinking about how to implement strategies could all be a part of your support group agenda.

❑ *Follow-through:* We encourage you to go beyond the covers of these books in pursuing ideas that are of interest to you. Check the references in Chapter 11 for possible resources and follow-up steps.

WHY ARE WE TAKING THIS TRIP?

In the first part of this chapter, you had a chance to examine some questions you may want answered. In addition to the answers to these questions, we would like to paint a broader picture of the purposes of these books. We are on this trail because:

❑ *Increased awareness:* During the past decades, there has been a growing awareness of the environment around us and how it is being degraded. People have become increasingly concerned that the survival of civilization depends on the development of an environmental ethic—and of behaviors that support that ethic. The Three Mile Islands and Love Canals of the 70s, the Bhopal chemical spill in India, the Exxon-Valdez oil spill in Alaska in the 80s, the Kuwait oil fires in the 90s, the more recent BP oil spill in the Gulf of Mexico, and the Fukushima nuclear meltdown in Japan are reminders of the urgent need to care for the environment. Many individuals consider global climate change as one of the most threatening problems facing the planet today. What are the best ways for teachers, parents, youth group facilitators, and outdoor leaders to address these issues?

Over the past several years, we have also witnessed a booming interest in exploring the world within each of us – the human brain and how we learn. The past decades were filled with programs promoting personal growth, coping with life transitions, lifelong learning, and changing lifestyles. People today are experiencing strong interest in understanding and exploring the universe within them.

❑ *Personal needs:* Many young people, and adults alike, are experiencing some confusion in their lives. In the face of accelerating change and future shock, almost everyone is dealing with questions in value areas, such as technology, friendship, work, leisure, money, family, love, religion, future, and many others.

Accompanying this confusion may be a sense of devaluation. Anyone who has worked with young people is aware that many of them have a relatively low estimate of their worth. They seem to lack self-confidence and often wrestle with issues of competence. Research shows that low self-confidence has a direct bearing on school achievement, task performance, and employment success. There is a strong need to help young people and adults enhance their self-esteem and to clarify their values in this area in order to create healthier lifestyles.

❑ *Societal needs:* We are facing and will continue to face oppressive social issues, such as racism, sexism, ageism, homophobia, hunger, poverty, and war. Many individuals would agree that the U.S. is a divided nation, not a united nation. The proper task for camps, schools, and other social institutions is to tackle some of these societal needs through well-planned activities, both indoors and outdoors, and to plan staff development sessions to improve their knowledge in these areas.

❑ *Institutional challenge:* Human service agencies and programs are at a turning point. As we continue in the 21st century, the question of how to respond to critical personal and social needs faces us. Are we incorporating goals, such as character building, raising self-esteem, democratic decision making, civic participation, cooperative strategies, conflict resolution, and values clarification into our programs and curricula?

THE SYNERGISTIC SYNTHESIS

How do we respond to the current needs? How can we tap the energy that people have for exploring their internal and external environments? How can we help people develop the tools to respond to personal and societal needs? How can we support institutions that are facing the challenges of the future?

We believe that part of the answer to these questions lies in the concepts of synergy and synthesis. Synergy is the joint action of separate parts in such a way that the results are greater than the effects of the parts acting alone. Another way to explain this concept is that sometimes, 1 + 1 can equal more than 2. Synthesis is the combining of two or more parts into a whole. The concepts of synergistic synthesis apply to the fields of outdoor, environmental, and humanistic education.

When we combine the fields, as we have done in these two books, we have magnified the possibilities that humanizing education will meet some personal and social needs. These two fields, which continue to grow, can complement each other. Goals, principles, and applications from each form a natural bridge. Together, they become powerful allies in meeting individual and institutional challenges for the future.

OUTDOOR AND ENVIRONMENTAL EDUCATION

(*Terminology note: Over the years, some of the titles of this field have evolved and changed. Among the terms that have resulted are nature study, camping education, outdoor education, environmental education, outdoor recreation, ecological education, adventure education, earth education, experiential education, place-based education, and many more. The authors have compiled a list of 78 related terms. We have chosen to use "Outdoor and Environmental Education" for convenience and clarity.)

Camp leaders, teachers, school administrators, recreation leaders, coaches, naturalists, outdoor educators, and other helping professionals have planted many seeds in developing the fields of outdoor and environmental education. For our purpose in these books, we view these fields very broadly. We believe that this profession embraces the following ideas:

❏ Outdoor and environmental education is a process that utilizes a wide variety of learning resources, both indoors and outdoors. Outdoor learning activities can be coordinated with and complement indoor activities.

❏ Outdoor and environmental education is multidisciplinary in nature. As a means of curriculum enrichment, it applies to many subject matter areas on the elementary, secondary, and college levels.

❏ Outdoor and environmental education, as a means of understanding natural and person-made environments, is a continuous, life-long process.

❏ Outdoor and environmental education uses teaching methods and techniques, based on a philosophy of experience-based, active learning through direct contact in the community and natural areas. This endeavor involves exploration and problem-solving, along with drawing on the senses of touch, taste, smell, sight, and hearing to the fullest possible extent.

❏ Such activities encourage the development of skills, attitudes, values, and concepts focusing on interrelationships. Human beings are seen as a part of the natural environment, and not apart from it. Interdependence and diversity are important concepts in this field.

❏ Knowledge of the out-of-doors can have a significant carryover value for leisure-time and recreational enrichment.

❑ Outdoor and environmental education will become increasingly important as this nation becomes more urbanized and technologized. Planning and decision-making, with regard to the proper care of the environment, will rest with all the citizens of the nation. In order to help participants develop citizenship skills, we need to create programs that:

❑ Facilitate growth in awareness, mindfulness, understanding, and appreciation of our surroundings.

❑ Demonstrate concern for improving communication, effective group dynamics, and human relations skills.

❑ Encourage the expression of personal values and ideas about the human and natural environments, respect diversity of beliefs, and help participants clarify values.

❑ Create an atmosphere or climate that invites environmental awareness and lifestyle changes in sustainable and ecological directions.

❑ Respect people for their positive qualities and verbally validate them.

❑ Encourage trust, caring, empathy, cooperation, and risk-taking through structured experiences and modeling supportive behavior.

❑ Structure opportunities for participant involvement in planning, problem solving, and evaluating the learning experience.

❑ Provide for differences in participants' needs, interests, abilities, and learning styles by offering a variety of formats and content areas.

❑ Build in opportunities for individuals and groups to have successful and joyful experiences in the environment.

❑ Help people overcome blocks to learning about the natural/human environment, while allowing them to take more responsibility for their own growth.

HUMANISTIC EDUCATION

Growing out of the work of Abraham Maslow, Carl Rogers, Louis Raths, Arthur W. Combs, Howard Kirschenbaum, Jack Canfield, Gerald Weinstein, Sidney Simon, Merrill Harmin and others, the results of humanizing education have touched thousands of camps, schools and other institutions across the country. The philosophy underlying this approach has struck a chord in people who want to maintain their humanity in the face of some depersonalizing conditions. Perhaps, the major reason for the rapid growth of the field is the fact that the philosophy can be implemented by many practical and intentional strategies. This humanistic approach is based upon a number of assumptions about people and learning, including the following:

❏ It is important to address the "whole person" in any educational endeavor. In addition to cognitive learning, it is crucial that we acknowledge the affective areas of human experience. The two areas cannot be separated as we learn.

❏ People learn best when they feel safe, respected, appreciated, motivated, and challenged, when they have opportunities to make choices in their lives, and when they have chances to identify and build on their own strengths and interests.

❏ There is a universe within each of us that is a legitimate and exciting subject matter for exploration. Humanistic education seeks to help people develop self-scientist skills—learning by reflection from our own thoughts, feelings, and behaviors.

❏ We must help people develop a sense of identity, a sense of connectedness, and a sense of mastery or locus of control. Identity involves one's self-image and feelings of self-worth (e.g., "Who am I? What do I stand for, value, and believe in?"). Connectedness involves one's relationship with other people (e.g., "How do I relate to other people? With whom do I belong?"). Mastery or locus of control involves the extent to which one is in charge of what happens to him (e.g., "How can I affect and direct the flow of my life?").

❏ We must create learning environments that encourage pluralism and respect for differences, collaboration and cooperation, nourishment and support among people, and opportunities to generate alternative solutions to problems.

❏ Learning will be internalized to a greater extent when both the experiential (actively participating) and reflective (relating to one's own life experience) modes are employed; different learning styles are incorporated in the program (e.g., listening, observing, reading, touching, discussing, note-taking, playing, working alone, and working cooperatively with a group).

❑ Humanistic education is an approach to creating positive learning climates that encourage people to develop *life skills* that they find valuable in addressing personal and societal concerns. Humanistic education helps people develop life skills in four areas: the cognitive (thinking), the affective (feeling), the active (behaving), and the interpersonal (human relations).

❑ Cognitive skills include choosing freely (e.g., dealing with peer pressure); developing awareness of available alternatives; choosing with an awareness of the consequences of one's choices; being aware of patterns in one's life; thinking critically (e.g., analyzing, synthesizing, inferring); and ideating (being able to generate ideas and alternatives).

❑ Affective skills include identifying and acknowledging feelings as one source in making decisions; legitimizing one's intuition as another possible source; focusing on what one prizes and cherishes; empathizing with other people's feelings; and enhancing self-esteem.

❑ Active skills include acting on one's choices (moving from awareness and insight to behavioral change); goal-setting, as well as culling out the inconsistencies between what one would like to do and what one is likely to do.

❑ Interpersonal skills include publicly affirming one's choices, where appropriate; active listening; resolving conflict situations; asking clarifying questions; cooperating in work and play; and validating (focusing on the "positive" in self and others, and communicating appreciations).

WHAT LIES AHEAD ON THE TRAIL?

Based on the aforementioned guidelines and principles, this book and its companion book (*201 Nature and Human Nature Activities*) take a humanistic approach to outdoor and environmental education. They will help people learn life skills for enhancing the quality of their lives, the quality of their communities, and the quality of the natural environment.

Accordingly, the book you hold in your hands is organized in four sections:

❑ *Why?* Chapter 1 examines the need for this book, some possible reasons for your picking it up, and our reasons for writing it.

❑ How? Chapter 2 explores the goals, principles, and foci around which you can humanize and environmentalize your program.

❑ *Who? What?* Chapters 3 through 10 offer interviews and a case study with some of the cutting-edge leaders in the field. These "inner-views" answer some of the following questions: Who has been implementing these activities, values, principles, and goals?

What do their beliefs and philosophies look like? What have they learned by studying and creating successful programs and movements around the world? Chapter 10 offers a bevy of quotations to further jump-start your thinking.

❏ *Where?* Where do you turn if you are interested in going beyond this book? Chapter 11 details references for many resourceful people, books, periodicals, and organizations that could provide follow-up support. It also offers a peek at *201 Nature and Human Nature Activities*. Our hope is that our two books will be a springboard for further exploration.

"How shall we come to terms with nature? How shall we come to terms with our own kind?"

—Stuart Chase

GIVING CREDIT WHERE CREDIT IS DUE

We thank Dr. Sidney Simon for his IALAC story that we adapted in this chapter. He has been our mentor in many areas of humanistic education, and we are grateful for his guidance.

In the field of humanistic education, we are forever indebted to the giants on whose shoulders we stand ... including Sid Simon, Louis Raths, Howie Kirschenbaum, Merrill Harmin, Leland Howe, and Gerry Weinstein.

CHAPTER 2
DESIGNING YOUR PROGRAM OR CURRICULUM

Rawpixel/iStock/Thinkstock

"Good education provides a sense of community, personal identity, inner strength, purpose, meaning, and belonging."

—John Goodlad

The intended goals of your organization or school are the foundation upon which the program and curriculum are built. Goals need to be consistent with each other and be attainable with the human and natural resources available. The program or curriculum should reflect these goals in every way. Creative programming is the process of putting together the elements of successful activities in new ways in order to accomplish desired goals.

BROAD GOALS AND PHILOSOPHY

The main purpose for providing participants with an outdoor and environmental experience is to enrich their total education. The learning environment becomes the forest, field, stream or lake, city block, neighborhood, or mountaintop. The use of each of these built and natural ecosystems should be maximized because this is a prime opportunity for firsthand learning.

Every contact throughout the day is viewed as an educational opportunity (including the tasks of daily living, if participants stay overnight in a residential setting). The program or curriculum encompasses all that happens to participants. We learn from all of our experiences with the environment, whether in a formal class, structured or unstructured activity, or talking informally with someone. A broad view of what constitutes a learning experience is essential in humanizing outdoor and environmental education.

A sampling of goals you might consider in designing your program or curriculum includes the following:

❑ Goal #1: Understanding Yourself and Others

Gaining more understanding of yourself and others is a lifelong goal. Exposure to new environments often stimulates new insights in both of these areas. Immersion with people and nature, especially in a camp setting, can spark knowledge of self and others. Planned activities can be aimed at helping participants cooperate, show empathy, share attitudes and values, and think and act positively toward themselves and others.

❑ Goal #2: Respecting and Enjoying the Environment

Our environment is our heritage to preserve, change, or destroy. An important goal of the program should be to encourage participants to respect and enjoy nature and person-made environments, whether close to home or far away. One way to do this is to gather staff and other participants who model their values of appreciation and respect for all living things.

Examples of wise use and abuse of our environment are all around us. The only rational choice is to live in ways that assure our survival and the preservation of our surroundings. Planned activities should be woven with the threads of care and concern for preserving the natural world wherever possible.

Informal learning opportunities must also relate the same message in both direct and subtle ways. Care must be taken to conserve food, put out campfires, pick up litter, release captured animals, remove only plants that occur in abundance, plant trees, improve trails, and do other service projects to maintain and improve the area. We must encourage an ethic of care for living on our planet.

❑ Goal #3: Living Safely and Healthfully Outdoors

Human health and safety are very important outdoors because of the dangerous accidents that can occur. With the increase in leisure time in our society and the growing popularity of outdoor activities, everyone needs to know how to survive without serious illness or accidents. Precautions to be taken in various activities can best be learned while doing them. Safety skills taught in the context of hiking, canoeing, fishing, fire building, sleeping out, shelter building, or eating off of the land are much more meaningful than a video or textbook approach.

❑ Goal #4: Developing Lifelong Outdoor and Environmental Interests

This goal of developing lifelong outdoor and environmental interests is possible only if a person has the skills and attitudes necessary for enjoying the natural environment. The exposure to activities, such as hiking, bird watching, natural crafts, creative writing, stream exploration, or whatever outdoor experiences the program provides, could lead to future hobbies and pastimes. The true test of the value of an educational experience is what effect it has on the lifestyle of the participant.

The aforementioned broad goals can be adapted or expanded to meet the purpose of various organizations and institutions. The important point to remember is that the goals form the springboard from which your program or curriculum is launched.

Take some time now to modify and/or expand on these goals. What long-range visions do you have for your own program or curriculum?

SOME PRINCIPLES OF CREATIVE PROGRAMMING

A principle is a statement of an ideal condition for implementing goals. Principles serve as a checklist for determining if the program's content and process are being directed to your goals. They serve as guideposts along the way to providing a humanistic journey.

❑ Principle #1: Respect and Support

If the staff does not like and respect the participants, it will be difficult to reach any of the goals. An attitude of support is crucial if participants are to feel safe enough to take risks, learn, and grow.

❑ Principle #2: Blending

The staff should have an adequate background in outdoor skills, environmental values, and human relations skills. A delicate blend of knowledge in these areas is necessary in order to effectively implement the program or curriculum.

❑ Principle #3: Realistic Goals

The program or curriculum should reflect realistic goals and be attainable within the available time and resources. Not only should the goals be realistic and well-suited to the participants, but the activities should also be clearly focused to accomplish a desired goal(s).

❑ Principle #4: Understanding Values

The staff should understand their own values and those of the participants, before (and while) the program or curriculum is implemented. It is important that the staff is willing to clarify their own values before attempting to work with participants and their values.

❑ Principle #5: Holistic View

The program should be viewed as a totality and include such components as introductory community-building, ongoing maintenance of a sense of community, activities for closure, and evaluation. This principle stresses the importance of being aware of the developmental phases of any group or community-building effort.

❑ Principle #6: Adequate Time

The staff should have time to plan together, as well as to build personal relationships. A smoothly operating community doesn't just happen. Adequate planning time must be allotted to coordinating activities. The staff must devote time on a regular basis to knowing and caring for each other, to resolving conflicts, and to solving problems and concerns that emerge.

❑ Principle #7: Evaluation

Ongoing evaluation may be the most discussed and the least-applied of all the programming advice given. Evaluation is the best means of knowing how to modify activities to better accomplish goals.

PROGRAM OR CURRICULUM FOCUS

Once the goals and principles have been defined and written down for clarity, the program or curriculum focus must be considered. The focus is the organizational mode or way of implementing the program or curriculum. Environmental and outdoor education foci have varied widely.

❑ Focus #1: Subject Matter Disciplines or Curriculum Approach

The most common focus used by schools conducting resident outdoor programs has been the subject matter or curriculum-centered approach. This focus organizes activities around traditional subject matter disciplines, such as science, mathematics, language arts, social studies, music, art, and physical education. More recently, educators have added technology and engineering to this list. The process of planning starts with the subject, such as science, and then examines some objectives of the science curriculum at a particular grade level. The next step is usually to select certain objectives that can be best learned outside of the school classroom.

A classic example of this approach is the pond ecology lesson. Most all science curricula contain objectives dealing with food chains and food webs in aquatic environments. Usually, educators conclude that the most efficient and meaningful way to learn about food chains and webs in aquatic environments is to visit a pond or stream and examine the organisms firsthand. Predator and prey relationships among the organisms often can be viewed while the organisms are still being collected.

❑ Focus #2: Problem-Solving Approach

This focus centers on a problem to be investigated. The activities and methods spring from the problem as it is solved. For example, one problem could be phrased, "What can be learned about the lives of people who lived in this area and about us from the evidence found in the cemetery?" With this problem-based learning approach, activities are designed to reveal answers and are not confined to any particular subject matter area. If done with care, rubbings with paper and crayons can be taken of the epitaphs, dates, and designs on the tombstones. Some of the old tombstones can provide examples of mechanical weathering and opportunities for rock identification. Participants can write their own autobiographies as epitaphs, and stories of what they would imagine life to be like in the past.

❑ Focus #3: Environmental Clean-Up Approach

This focus centers on particular issues in the area. Air pollution sources and its effects can be isolated, and action projects planned to reduce the problem. Litter surveys and pickups can be planned, and methods to prevent future littering explored. There are many community issues that can be explored in this way.

❑ Focus #4: Adventure Programs and Outdoor Challenge Skills

Adventure programs provide participants with practical experiences in survival skills, such as camping, mountain climbing and rappelling, fire building, pitching a tent, outdoor cooking, and other camping skills, as well as lifetime sports, such as archery, fishing and casting, and skiing. Skill development, along with self and group understanding, are the primary purposes of this approach. Outward Bound and the National Leadership School are examples of this focus.

❑ Focus #5: Nature and Ecological Awareness

This focus concentrates upon a wide variety of structured activities aimed at increasing environmental awareness and mindfulness. The five senses are used extensively, as well as the introduction of ecological concepts and games to explore various types of ecosystems. The flow learning approach of Joseph Cornell is an example of this focus and is described in Chapter 4.

❑ Focus #6: Natural History and Identification

This focus concentrates heavily upon people learning the common and/or scientific names and important characteristics of flora and fauna. Knowing the name of a plant, as well as where it grows, its fruit, bud, leaf, and flower characteristics, and the uses to people are important in this focus. The Audubon Summer Camps are examples of this focus.

❑ Focus #7: The Location as the Key to Learning About the Environment

This focus depends upon a particular location or place to teach environmental concepts, skills, and values. Sometimes, these programs use parks, school sites, vacant lots, sanctuaries, or even city streets as the contexts for activities. On occasion, participants travel to specific locations for extensive periods of time to learn about these places firsthand. There have been many place-based education programs developed recently to expand the participants' knowledge of where they live and how their community functions.

❑ Focus #8: Personal Growth Through Outdoor Experiences

This focus uses the outdoors and environmental values issues to help participants grow in interpersonal and self-understanding. The outdoor setting and outdoor adventure skills and expeditions are used as vehicles to personal growth and improved human relations. One example of this type of program is described in Chapter 9—Human Relations Youth Adventure Camp.

It may have become clear as you examined these eight program or curriculum emphases that very few appear in pure form in practice. Various combinations of foci are usually blended to best meet the goals and philosophy of a particular person or organization. No one structure will meet all goals equally well. No one focus is best for all outdoor and environmental staffs to implement. The important point is to be aware of the various foci and to combine them in creative ways to reach desired goals.

Take some time now to focus on your own program or curriculum. You might rank-order the foci in order of their importance in your own program. Or, you might think of practical applications for how you could integrate and combine them in your own program.

PROGRAM ACTIVITIES: WHETTING YOUR APPETITE

Once you have identified your goals, principles, and foci, it is time to generate and select specific, appropriate activities. If your staff conducts brainstorming sessions in planning the program, you can generate an endless number of activities. Pooling ideas not only serves to expand the number of program options, it acts as a means of sharing among the staff. Piggy-backing on the ideas of others results in many more activities than any individual staff member could generate alone.

One hundred program ideas resulting from brainstorming sessions of the staff of the Human Relations Youth Adventure Camp (see Chapter 9) are offered at this point, as an example of the wide variety of outdoor activities available for program planning. We hope that these will whet your appetite for the many humanizing activities described in our companion book, *201 Nature and Human Nature Activities* (see the Resources chapter in this book for more information):

❑ Design a banner, flag, or symbol representing your group using native materials.
❑ Burn names and symbols of everyone into a driftwood log or board.
❑ Write a guide booklet for a self-made nature trail.
❑ Choose quiet spots for individuals to use for solo reflection.
❑ Make nature crafts to exchange on a bartering day.

- ❏ Carve walking sticks with notches or symbols of new experiences gained.
- ❏ Provide notebooks for everyone to keep daily journals.
- ❏ Form backrub chains, when people are tired and sore.
- ❏ Do community service projects, such as building a bridge, campfire log circle, outhouse pit, trail clearing, sauna, etc.
- ❏ Build sandcastles on the beach.
- ❏ Build a raft and float down the stream or across the lake.
- ❏ Spend 24 hours in the woods alone.
- ❏ Make bread, pie, or jam for everyone from berries you pick.
- ❏ Make new obstacle challenges for the group-initiative ropes course.
- ❏ Eat a meal blindfolded, while being fed by a partner.
- ❏ Set up a board for everyone to share favorite quotes, proverbs, or sayings.
- ❏ Set up a schedule for an all-night fire vigil.
- ❏ Invent a new ceremony to increase environmental awareness and then do it.
- ❏ Lead a session in body exercises related to movements of nature.
- ❏ Tell a round-robin story around the campfire.
- ❏ Read the group a story about a topic related to the environment or a famous naturalist.
- ❏ Do values clarification activities related to the interests and concerns of participants.
- ❏ Invent new games of cooperation and communication.
- ❏ Find out what skills and talents participants have that they would lead for others.
- ❏ Make a tree house or an underground fort.
- ❏ Lead a guided fantasy, pretending to travel inside the vessels of a tree.
- ❏ Go on a night walk without flashlights.
- ❏ Walk down the center of a stream in sneakers as a group.
- ❏ Conduct a '50s or '60s night.
- ❏ Make nature collages, showing how you feel about this environment.
- ❏ Take an early morning "polar bear" dip in the lake or stream.
- ❏ Prepare and serve everyone a special meal.
- ❏ Paint each other's faces and bodies with watercolors.
- ❏ Write a community newspaper about shared experiences.
- ❏ Conduct a public interview with different people each day.
- ❏ Invite someone from the surrounding community to dinner.
- ❏ Have a goodwill day in which everyone exchanges good deeds.
- ❏ Eat a meal similar to that served in another culture.
- ❏ Change your personality for one hour to understand how it feels.
- ❏ Put on a circus.
- ❏ Don't talk for a day.

- ❑ Don't eat or drink for a day.
- ❑ Blindfold yourself for a day.
- ❑ Take a beeline compass hike to a specific place.
- ❑ Conduct a creativity-sharing night.
- ❑ Make boats from found materials and race them in a stream.
- ❑ Build shelters from natural materials.
- ❑ Watch the sunrise and sunset.
- ❑ Dig for artifacts at an abandoned farm (get permission first).
- ❑ Go mountain climbing or rappelling.
- ❑ Spend time writing creatively and sharing what is written.
- ❑ Use cornhusks to make crafts.
- ❑ Make nature mobiles.
- ❑ Paint rocks with designs that have personal meanings.
- ❑ Dye wool with natural plant dyes.
- ❑ Make candles and soap.
- ❑ Make macramé jewelry.
- ❑ Make and fire clay beads.
- ❑ Have a non-thumb day (tape everyone's thumb down).
- ❑ Go jogging in the morning together.
- ❑ Explore a local cemetery to learn history.
- ❑ Dress up in a crazy costume.
- ❑ Go on a scavenger hunt with a partner.
- ❑ Make a group weaving, paint a group picture, or write a group poem.
- ❑ Have a strength bombardment session to tell people what their strengths are.
- ❑ Sketch nature pictures.
- ❑ Do sun prints.
- ❑ Write a letter to yourself and mail it home.
- ❑ Exchange handmade gifts.
- ❑ Conduct camping skills sessions on knife sharpening, ax use, fire building, whittling, or wood splitting.
- ❑ Find shapes and characters in the constellations at night and rename them.
- ❑ Invent and make wooden toys.
- ❑ Sleep out on top of a mountain.
- ❑ Collect, wax, and polish driftwood.
- ❑ Do nature-awareness activities.

- Invite people to share their knowledge.
- Hold a service auction, where everyone offers a service.
- Talk to trees, rocks, and other objects, and imagine what they would say back to you.
- Hug and dance with trees.
- Move your body like trees in the wind, clouds moving across the sky, and raindrops falling in a puddle.
- Invent games using found items, such as branches, stones, grasses, leaves, or acorns.
- Find objects in nature containing successively higher numbers (e.g., plant with one leaf, two leaves, etc.).
- Create a giant sculpture using rocks or logs.
- Create a sculpture using people—form different animals, plants, or buildings.
- Go on a litter hunt to see how large a pile of litter can be built (and then throw it away).
- Pretend people are raindrops falling to earth and follow the paths the water would take.
- Role-play earthworms, birds, snakes, insects, and other animals, as well as inanimate objects, such as rocks, fences, tires, houses, or telephone poles.
- Find familiar shapes in the clouds and in the spaces between tree branches.
- Make a nest like a bird.
- Make paintbrushes from pine needles, weeds, and other natural objects, and paint a picture.
- Search the area for "Guinness world records" for the fattest tree, prettiest insect, or biggest acorn.
- Find lines (zig-zag, vertical, parallel, lattice, wavy, horizontal, slanted) and shapes (spirals, circles, triangles, and ellipses) in nature and the built-environment.
- Invent solutions to practical problems by getting ideas from nature.
- Pick up natural objects and see how many questions can be asked about each one.
- On a sunny day, play tag with each other's shadows.
- Go out in the rain and get wet (not during a thunderstorm).
- Role in a pile of leaves and "wash" your hands in a leaf bath.
- See how many people can fit on a section of sidewalk or stump.
- Dig the deepest hole you can in the ground.
- Do something to improve the environment.

Dr. John Dewey, considered the father of experiential education, wrote about educative or worthwhile experiences in *Experience & Education* (1938). He stressed the importance of activities that encouraged meaningful growth toward attaining life skills and continuous learning.

Examine the aforementioned list of 100 brainstormed activities to identify those you think will lead to rewarding and enjoyable memories of nature and human nature. On your mark, get set, go!

> *"Let our children look at the mountains and the stars up above. Let them look at the beauty of the waters and the trees and flowers on earth. They will then begin to think, and to think is the beginning of a real education."*
>
> —David Polis

GIVING CREDIT WHERE CREDIT IS DUE

We acknowledge the following co-authors with Joel Goodman, who have explored the topic of evaluating the curriculum or program in their earlier humanistic education writings: Kenneth Huggins, Donald Read, and Sidney Simon.

We also thank the staff of the Human Relations Youth Adventure Camp for brainstorming the list of 100 activities that appear in this chapter.

CHAPTER 3
TWO VIEWS OF THE NEW NATURE MOVEMENT

"A child's world is fresh and new and beautiful, full of wonder and excitement. It is our misfortune that for most of us, that clear-eyed vision, that true instinct for what is beautiful and awe-inspiring, is dimmed and even lost before we reach adulthood."

—Rachel Carson

Ingram Publishing/Thinkstock

We are currently at a time in history when our planet faces serious threats, such as global warming; contamination of oceans, freshwater, soil, and air; over-dependence upon fossil fuels; water shortages; chemical spills on land and water; rainforest destruction; nuclear plant meltdowns; mountaintop removal for coal; and many more human-caused disasters. With increasing urban populations, people are becoming separated and alienated from nature and losing their emotional connection with the land. In response to this critical situation, many people are playing activist and advocacy roles in promoting a deeper connection between nature and human nature. Two people who have contributed greatly to this cause are Dr. Cheryl Charles and Richard Louv.

Cheryl has a long career as a proponent for connecting children and nature. She is an innovator, author, organizational executive, and educator. She is the co-founder, president and CEO emerita of the Children & Nature Network (C&NN), where she coordinates its international activities. Recipient of numerous awards for her leadership, she was the founding national director of the pioneering K-12, interdisciplinary environment education programs, Project Learning Tree and Project WILD. Cheryl is also research scholar and founding executive director of the Nature Based Leadership Institute at Antioch University New England (AUNE). In this position, she promotes the vision of a world in which all humans live, learn, serve, and lead in healthy balance with the natural world.

Rich is a co-founder and chairman emeritus of the C&NN and widely acclaimed author of a trilogy of nature-related books. These landmark books are directed at combating nature-deficit disorder, a term he coined to describe the widespread human alienation from the natural world. His first book in this trilogy, *Last Child in the Woods* (2005), was a national bestseller and was revised and expanded in 2008. He compiled the results of many studies pointing to nature contact as essential for healthy child development. His second book, *The Nature Principle*, issues a call to action to adults, and his third book, *Vitamin N*, provides 500 ways to enrich the health and happiness of families and communities. In 2008, he was awarded the coveted Audubon Medal to recognize his outstanding achievement in the field of conservation and environmental protection. He is currently working on his tenth book about the evolving relationship between humans and other animals.

In this interview you will learn more about the C&NN, some key research findings related to the benefits of nature contacts, and the current global status of the new nature movement.

- Cliff: The Children & Nature Network (C&NN) has played an important role in growing what has been called the "new nature movement." What evidence have you seen that this movement is alive and well today?
- Rich: In the U.S., there's been progress among state legislatures, schools and businesses, civic organizations, and government agencies. Family nature clubs (multiple families that agree to show up for a hike) are proliferating. Regional campaigns are bringing people from across political, religious, and economic

divides, to connect children to nature. In September 2012, the World Congress of the International Union for the Conservation of Nature (IUCN) cited "adverse consequences for both healthy child development ('nature-deficit disorder'), as well as responsible stewardship for nature and the environment in the future," and then passed a resolution titled "The Child's Right to Connect with Nature and to a Healthy Environment." This connection is, indeed, a human right and the acknowledgement of that is progress.

For more promising trends, the following is a blog post I wrote on the past year: http://www.childrenandnature.org/2015/12/31/the-7-best-stories-and-trends-of-2015-for-children-families-communities-and-nature-it-was-a-very-good-year/.

- Cheryl: There are many indicators that the new nature movement, including the movement to reconnect children with nature, is alive and well. Since the founding of the C&NN in 2006, following the publication of Richard Louv's landmark *Last Child in the Woods*, Rich and I have made it a practice to look for indicators that the movement is gaining traction. We have not done a comprehensive analysis, but have looked for signs. Examples include: the phenomenal increase in the number of nature-based preschools and kindergartens; the increased media attention; growth in the research base, with increased studies focusing on the benefits to children from nature-based experiences; explicit incorporation of key messages about the importance of connecting children with nature by a variety of notable environmental organizations, such as the International Union for the Conservation of Nature, The Nature Conservancy, the National Audubon Society, the National Wildlife Federation, The Trust for Public Lands and others, as well as health organizations, such as the American Academy of Pediatrics; and the growing frequency of international interest from people in nations throughout the world. One measure, for example, is that people from more than 200 countries have visited the C&NN website at www.childrenandnature.org and people from more than 100 nations have downloaded one or more of C&NN's free publications.

- Cliff: In 2006, the mission of C&NN was to build a strong movement to connect children and nature. Has this mission changed over the last few years? If so, how?

- Rich: The mission has remained the same, but we've expanded our reach by creating more initiatives, such as creating nature-rich cities, transforming schoolyards, and natural libraries.

- Cheryl: The core mission of the C&NN has not changed. It remains the only organization solely focused on connecting children with nature for their health and well-being and that of the Earth itself.

- Cliff: The C&NN has developed a comprehensive collection of research, organized according to the benefits of increased nature contacts. What are some of these benefits, and how are they reflected in practice?

- Rich: The research has greatly expanded over the last few years. It tends to point in one direction: experiences in the natural world appear to offer great benefits to psychological and physical health, and the ability to learn, for children and adults. The research strongly suggests that time in nature can help many children learn to build confidence in themselves; reduce the symptoms of attention deficit hyperactivity disorder; calm children and help them focus.

A relatively new body of evidence strongly suggests that the natural world increases physical competency linked to mental acuity; increases the ability to see patterns, where others see chaos; stimulates the senses to collect and perceive knowledge and apply it; and increases creativity. Several studies show that children who play in natural settings are more cooperative and inclusive in their play, and more likely to create their own games than those who play on flat turf or asphalt playgrounds.

Without independent play, the critical cognitive skill called executive function is at risk. Executive function is a complex process, but at its core is the ability to exert self-control, to control and direct emotion and behavior. Children develop executive function, in large part, through make-believe play. The function is aptly named: when you make up your own world, you're the executive. In 2001, researchers replicated a study on self-regulation done in the 1940s. Psychologist Elena Bodrova at Mid-Continent Research for Education and Learning explained the results: "Today's five-year-olds were acting at the level of three-year-olds 60 years ago, and today's seven-year-olds were barely approaching the level of a five-year-old 60 years ago. So the results were very sad." A child's executive function, as it turns out, is a better predictor of success in school than IQ.

- Cheryl: It is correct that C&NN has developed a comprehensive collection of research that includes studies related to the various benefits associated with children's and adults' contact with nature. Importantly, C&NN's research library and related resources continue to grow and are regularly updated. Since the C&NN began publishing its volumes of annotated research, there has been a notable increase in the number of studies generally related to positive outcomes for children from nature-based experiences. In examining the reported findings, most of the studies continue to be correlational, not causal. I have summarized the benefits as indicating that children tend to be "happier, healthier, and smarter," when they have nature-based experiences in their lives. Do we know how much is needed, of what kinds of experiences, with what frequency? We do not. We do know that there is ample evidence to indicate a variety of benefits.

Children tend to have enhanced self-confidence, creativity, problem-solving ability, and collaborative skills when they have the cumulative experience of independent play and learning in nature-based settings in the outdoors. There are studies that indicate that test scores in subject and skill areas after nature-based experiences are as good as or better than the scores of children without that exposure. Children tend to be more physically active when outdoors in nature than when indoors, and physical activity is associated with healthy weights and other positive health attributes. There are also studies that indicate the importance of informal learning through play and exploration in nature for an emotional sense of connection to nature and motivation to protect it. Tomorrow's caregivers of the Earth, informed and passionate conservationists, are today's children with deep connections to the living world. To gain these and other benefits, nature-based experiences need to be prioritized in children's lives—where they live, learn, play, and grow.

- Cliff: Both of you have published and spoken thousands of words about connecting people to the natural world. How have these experiences helped you grow in understanding the status of nature education around the world?

- Rich: Through research for my books, as well as traveling and speaking in many different countries, I have learned that this is a widespread issue. Particularly in developed countries, the gap between children and nature has been growing for at least three decades. But, it is occurring anywhere where people are migrating into cities. Since *Last Child in the Woods* was published in 2005, what I would consider the first denatured generation has entered adulthood. At the same time, a new mythology of technology is suggesting that nature doesn't matter anymore. We even hear talk of the "transhuman" or "posthuman" era in which people are optimally enhanced by technology. A proactive approach is simply part of today's reality. Getting kids outside needs to be a conscious act on the part of parents, pediatricians, educators, and other caregivers.

- Cheryl: To write and speak, one has to have something to say. And having something to say depends on experience, observation, reflection, and study. It is a privilege to be an observer and voice for the health and well-being of children, families, communities, and the environment that sustains us all. Am I as effective as I would like to be? No. Am I going to keep trying? Yes.

Jupiterimages/Stockbyte/Thinkstock

- Cliff: Richard has coined the term, "nature-deficit disorder" to describe humanity's growing alienation from nature. How effective has this phrase been in communicating your message?

- Rich: As young people spend less of their lives in natural surroundings, their senses narrow, physiologically and psychologically. Added to that, the over-organized childhood and the devaluing of unstructured play have huge implications for children's ability to self-regulate. This reduces the richness of human experience and contributes to a condition I call "nature-deficit disorder." I created that term to serve as a catchphrase to describe what many of us believe are the human costs of alienation from nature. Among them: diminished use of the senses, attention difficulties, higher rates of physical and emotional illnesses, a rising rate of myopia, child and adult obesity, vitamin D deficiency, and other maladies. Science has correlated experiences in the natural world with improvements in every one of these conditions. Obviously, nature-deficit disorder is not a medical diagnosis, though one might think of it as a condition of society. People know it when they see it, which may account for how quickly it entered several languages.
- Cheryl: I am deeply grateful to Rich for coining "nature-deficit disorder." With his seminal book, *Last Child in the Woods*, he startled the world with the graphic image of children's disconnect from their birthright and gave voice to the urgent need to reconnect children with nature. The term has been so effective that it helped to launch this worldwide movement, and is now widely used. It is fair to say that we are still deeply troubled by the numbers of children and families who do not experience healthy, nature-based environments in their daily lives.
- Cliff: The increase of digital technologies has helped and hindered the human connection to nature. What advice do you have for nature leaders and teachers about their use?
- Rich: Today, children and adults who work and learn in a dominating digital environment expend enormous energy *blocking out* many of the human senses—including ones we don't even know we have—in order to focus narrowly on the screen in front of the eyes. That's the very definition of being less alive. What parent wants his or her child to be less alive? Who among us wants to be less alive?

    The point here is not to be against technology, which offers us many gifts, but to find balance – and to give our children and ourselves an enriched life and a nature-rich future. In *The Nature Principle*, I include a section on what I call "techno-naturalists." I point out that taking technology with us into nature isn't new. A fishing rod, a compass, and binoculars are examples of technologies we've used for nature exploration. Today, the family that goes geocaching or wildlife photographing with their digital cameras is doing something as legitimate as backpacking; these gadgets offer an excuse to get outside.

    The attitude of young citizen naturalists toward technology is bound to be different from that of many older people—and that could be an advantage. However, I'm not keen on the kind of gadgets that go over the line—to the point where we become more aware of the gadget than of nature. iPod-guided tours of natural areas, for example, offer audio information at the cost of the use of many other senses. The litmus test for some of this technology should be how long it

Humanizing Outdoor and Environmental Education

takes for someone to look up from the screen, or forget the gadget, and actually experience nature, and to feel a sense of wonder. Another test is whether the technology is preventing other people from fully experiencing nature. Loud engines don't pass that test.

Technology does offer us many gifts. But electronic immersion, without a force to balance, drains the ability to pay attention, think clearly, and be productive and creative. The ultimate multitasking is to maximize the gifts of both the digital and the physical worlds, especially in nature—to develop what I've called "hybrid minds."

- Cheryl: Err on the side of caution. There is a place for technology, but it is not a substitute for direct experiences in nature.
- Cliff: Where do you see the "new nature movement" and the C&NN five years from now? Will it still exist and flourish in the future? Where do you see yourselves in five years?
- Rich: We're at a crucial point in what I call the new nature movement. Awareness has grown over the past decade, but we need to move more quickly into an action mode, whether we're parents, pediatricians, or mayors. We all can spend more time with children in nature. This is quite a challenge, one that emphasizes the importance of exploring nearby opportunities, particularly unstructured time in nature. Schedule outdoor time, direct experiences in nature; make getting outside in a natural area an intentional act—a healthful habit, if you will—that becomes part of your life. Ultimately, we need to accomplish deep cultural change; the objective is to give children the gifts of nature they deserve, and for all of us to find kinship with the lives around us, and wholeness in the lives we live.

One of the messages of my books is that conservation is no longer enough. Now we need to create nature. If we're going to have the biodiversity we need, we have to begin to transform our cities, yards, homes, and workplaces into incubators of biodiversity. That will hugely improve our psychological and physical health, our sense of pleasure and happiness, and our ability to learn. That's a very different image of the future than the one that is dominant now.

My book, *Vitamin N*, goes into some detail on how to achieve this on a city-by-city basis. Also, the National League of Cities (which represents 19,000 municipalities and 218 million Americans) and the C&NN announced a three-year partnership, the Cities Promoting Access to Nature initiative, to explore how municipalities can connect people with the natural world, where they live, work, learn, and play. We see the emergence of biophilic design of our homes and workplaces; reconciliation ecology and human/nature social capital; restorative homes and businesses; and ecopsychology and other forms of nature therapy. We see more citizen naturalists; nature-based schools; the Slow Food and simplicity movements; organic gardening; and urban agriculture, vanguard ranching and other forms of the new agrarianism. As these currents join, they'll lead us to a different view of the future – a nature-rich future. The barriers are still there, but I do believe there's more hope in the air, if you look for it.

- Cheryl: In five years, the new nature movement will be continuing to grow, expanding, inspiring, and demonstrating the benefits to humanity's health and well-being and that of all life from restoring, conserving, and enhancing healthy ecosystems of all kinds. The C&NN will be expanding its work as a network of networks, an ecology of people and organizations throughout the world, focused on connecting people of all ages with healthy natural environments in their everyday lives, and especially children. I imagine that Rich and I will still be doing everything we can to encourage and nourish this and other movements that are focused on developing healthy relationships with one another and the planet for generations to come. And, some of the time, he's likely to be fishing, and I will be in the woods and gardens playing and learning with my grandchildren, family, and friends.
- Cliff: Thank you both for thoughts on connecting nature and human nature. You have given us a great deal to think about before we act to make the world more livable.

> *"The purity of nature awakens the purity within ourselves."*
>
> —Dorothy Maclean

REFERENCES

See the chapter on "Mindfulness and Coming to Your Senses" in our companion book, *201 Nature and Human Nature Activities*, which is described at the beginning of the Resources chapter in this book.

CHAPTER 4

TRAVELING THE WORLD, BEARING NATURE'S GIFT OF PEACE

"When walking in nature, from the beauty around me I got my inspiration, from the silent receptiveness my meditation, and from the walking both my exercise and my breathing."

—Peace Pilgrim

Joseph Cornell is one of the most inspiring nature educators in the world. His first book, *Sharing Nature with Children*, helped spark a revolution in nature education, and it soon became a classic. His *Nature Awareness* books have been translated into 26 languages and are used by educators and nature enthusiasts all over the world. Joseph's book, *Listening to Nature*, inspired thousands of adults to deepen their relationships and experiences with the natural world.

He is the founder and director of Sharing Nature Worldwide, a popular *nature awareness* program for children and adults. In 1997, the Japanese Ministry of Education officially recognized Sharing Nature Japan (Nature Game Association) as a "public service corporation," a rare designation given to only a few widely recognized service groups.

Joseph Cornell has received many awards for his books and programs. He received the prestigious Honorary Award from the National Association of Interpretation "for his vast contribution to the field of natural science education." The Hungarian Society for Environmental Education awarded him with an Honorary Membership for his "service as a role model for educators worldwide." In 2001, he received an honorary doctoral degree from Unity College in Maine "for his illustrious career as a nature educator and writer." He also received the Countess Sonja-Bernadotte-Prize in Germany for his vast influence on environmental education in Central Europe.

His first book, *Sharing Nature with Children*, was selected by the U. S. Fish & Wildlife Service as one of the 15 most influential children and nature books published since 1890. Two of his books, *The Sky and Earth Touched Me* and Sharing Nature, were Indie Book Award Grand Prize Winners for all non-fiction. In 2011, Joseph was selected as one of the "100 biggest opinion leaders committed to the environment" by the French organization, Anges Gardiens de la Planete.

On a more personal note, I (Cliff Knapp) have had the pleasure of knowing Joseph for more than 32 years. I attended many of his nature programs and invited him to present workshops to my graduate students at Northern Illinois University. I have visited him at his home in Nevada City, California. We have also been on several workshop programs together, and he has been a guest in my home. I have collected his books, used them in my teaching, and recommended them to my students. He wrote the foreword for the first edition of our book, *Humanizing Environmental Education*, and Joel and I are honored to have his foreword in this updated book and its companion, *201 Nature and Human Nature Activities*.

More rewarding than reading his books is meeting him in person. He has a warm, comfortable personality, an infectious laugh, and a dynamic and energy-packed way of being with people. Once he introduces himself and the workshop agenda, his audiences are caught up into his enthusiasm and dedication to the field of nature education.

In the following interview, Joseph Cornell elaborates upon his work and explains why he believes his career has been so successful.

- Cliff: You have recently celebrated your 43rd year as a nature educator. What are some of the important changes in sharing nature that you have seen since you began?

- Joseph: The most positive changes I have seen are people feeling empowered to make a difference and the emphasis on our global community. The nature education field has matured in the sophistication of its programs, as well. Many more educators and institutions are embracing experiential, intuitive ways of teaching. I feel it is essential that we share nature in deeply inspiring ways. Tanaka Shozo, the great Japanese pioneering naturalist, said, "The care of rivers is not a question of rivers but of the human heart."

- Cliff: What early experiences in your life implanted a love of nature in you and a desire to teach others about the natural world?

- Joseph: When I was five-years-old, I was in my backyard and looking intently upward into a thick fog, when all of a sudden, bursting through a gap in the fog, came a flock of pearl-white snow geese. It seemed as if the sky had given birth to them. Seeing the snow geese thrilled me deeply, and ever since I've wanted to immerse myself in nature. By the time I was 12, I was waking up every morning at dawn to run through the wildlands near my home.

- Cliff: You have traveled to 30 countries in the world to share nature with others. Where have you found the most enthusiasm for your approach to nature education?

- Joseph: I've found that the deepest appreciation for my work is in countries that understand things intuitively and with the heart. Science *describes* reality; intuition *perceives* life directly. Countries like Brazil, Japan, Slovenia, Taiwan, South Korea, Greece, and India are examples of nations that are more feeling-oriented.

  Sharing Nature uses experiential methods to help people understand the principles of ecology in scientific as well as philosophical or spiritual ways, so people from diverse cultures and nations have all responded quite positively to our program. In Japan, they say our nature activities are "very Japanese." In Greece, I was told, "They're very Greek."

  Today, I mostly travel to countries where we have strong Sharing Nature organizations, like Japan, Germany, Netherlands, Brazil, China, and South Korea. In Japan alone, there are 10,000 trained Sharing Nature leaders in 224 regional organizations.

- Cliff: Your books have been translated into 26 languages. Can you explain why your writings have been so popular all over the world?

- Joseph: The Sharing Nature books offer educators engaging, easy-to-use, and effective nature activities they can use successfully with their students. Besides teaching ecology creatively, these games help people experience a profound sense of joy, serenity, and belonging to the natural world. We also use an innovative outdoor teaching strategy called Flow Learning, which has been praised worldwide by educators and group facilitators. Flow Learning gives teachers and youth leaders a simple, structured way to guide students into their own direct experiences of nature. Through playful games that awaken the student's curiosity and enthusiasm, learning becomes fun, immediate, and dynamic, instead of static and secondhand. The students emerge with a living, fresh understanding and reverence for nature.

Ingram Publishing/Thinkstock

The four stages of the flow learning system are awaken enthusiasm, focus attention, direct experience, and share inspiration. Each stage serves as a way to present different nature games and activities in accordance with how people learn. In fact, I have organized much of the contents of my book, *Sharing Nature: Nature Awareness Activities for All Ages* in this way.

The initial stage of awakening enthusiasm engages people with focused experiences that are playful and active. It is my way of getting the group rapidly involved in hands-on and minds-on games. We usually laugh a lot during this beginning set of activities. The second stage focuses attention on one or more of their physical senses of touch, hearing, and sight. Through these carefully selected activities, participants become more calm, observant, and receptive to their surroundings. During the third stage of deeper and direct adventures into nature, learners fully enter into a greater sense of harmony and wonder with their place. These games help us discover an inner sense of love, understanding, and belonging. The last stage of sharing inspiration enables the participants to further bond with their group, share personal experiences, and reflect on the meaning of the activities. At this time the leader gets feedback from the group and can also share inspiring stories about environmental role models and others who have made a difference in the world of nature. To describe flow learning in simple terms, it is a way of sequencing and organizing nature activities that honors principles of good teaching and learning.

- Cliff: You teach nature workshops to adults from all walks of life. How have teachers responded to your message about the importance of teaching students to love nature and have fun, before trying to teach them about the facts of nature?

Humanizing Outdoor and Environmental Education

- Joseph: When I have been introducing the Sharing Nature program overseas, a common reaction among educators is surprise, then delight, as they discover that a way of teaching exists that goes beyond learning facts. Whether in Australia, China, or Scotland, the reaction has been extremely enthusiastic. In Brazil, our country coordinator, Rita, gave a workshop in the Amazon for professional ecotourism guides, some of whom had worked in the area for 40 years. Their attitude, at first, was that she had little to teach them. But after several Sharing Nature activities, a woman approached Rita and said with deep emotion, "You are helping me find the forest inside of me! We don't know the forest in this way!" A teacher in the Southwest once asked the children in his class to draw a picture of themselves. He recalled, "The American children completely covered the paper with a drawing of their body, but my Navajo students drew themselves differently. They made their bodies much smaller and included the nearby mountains, canyon walls, and dry desert washes. To the Navajo, the environment is as much a part of who they are as are their own arms and legs." The understanding that we are a part of something larger than ourselves is Nature's greatest gift. With it, our sense of identity expands and, by extension, so does our compassion for all things. Nurturing a love of nature is the goal of each Sharing Nature activity and all our programs.
- Cliff: What are three of your most powerful nature activities, and what do you think makes them so powerful?
- Joseph: There are so many great nature activities it is hard to choose only three. The following activities have become quite popular and well-loved all over the world:

✓ The *Unnature Trail* game focuses the attention of even restless children and turns them into enthusiastic observers. The game is played by placing human-made objects along one side of a trail, and having the children walk over the section of trail one at a time, trying to spot as many objects as they can. Some of the objects should blend in with the surroundings, like a nail, rubber band, or clothespin. One child said after playing this activity, "I saw a lizard blink thirteen feet away!"

✓ In an *Interview with Nature* activity, you look for a special rock, plant, or animal that has an interesting story to tell. You ask it questions like, "What events have you seen in your life? What is it like to live here? Is there something you would like to tell me?" People sometimes feel a little awkward at first, talking to something as if it were alive. But, very quickly they come to appreciate the fact that their rock or tree *has* a precious life of its own.

✓ The forte of the *Camera Game* activity is heightening people's perception. This activity is played with two people: one is the photographer, the other the camera. When the "photographer" taps the shoulder of the "camera" twice, the camera-person opens his or her eyes on a nearby scene. Then, after three to five seconds, the photographer taps the "camera's" shoulder once to close the camera's eyes. Because the camera-person looks for only a few seconds—before his mind begins to daydream—the impact of the "picture" is quite powerful. Players of the *Camera Game* have told me that they've retained a vivid memory of their pictures for five, even eight years afterwards. This game helps children and adults experience what it is like to truly *see*. This activity also gives the "photographer" the incentive to look for and share beauty with another person.

- Cliff: Everyone is not as enthusiastic about nature as you are. What have been some of your greatest challenges in teaching others and having them become motivated and involved in *sharing nature with children*?

- Joseph: My greatest challenges have come when I have been unable to create a positive and uplifting atmosphere for learning and interacting with nature. I have found, however, that when I've been able to use the playful and joyful Sharing Nature activities and the Flow Learning process, I have been able to work successfully with all kinds of groups. Stories, fun activities, and deeply meaningful and rewarding nature experiences all help to "win" children and adults over to the process by helping them overcome any restlessness or reservations they might have.

- Cliff: Both of us are fascinated by the wisdom of early naturalists, such as John Muir and Henry David Thoreau. In fact, you have written a book about one of them, *John Muir: My Life with Nature*. What have you learned from these pioneers?

- Joseph: The importance of a deep contact with the natural world. Each of these pioneers cultivated a profound personal relationship with nature. Because of this, both Muir and Thoreau had a huge impact on people's lives. Robert Underwood Johnson, a leading conservationist of Muir's day, spoke of the tremendous influence Muir had on everyone then. He said appreciatively, "Muir's writings and enthusiasm were the chief forces that inspired the conservation movement. All other torches were lighted from his."

- Cliff: When you plan "Sharing Nature" workshops, what do you consider when selecting and sequencing nature exercises and activities?

- Joseph: Ideally, I first look for natural features that will provide a compelling experience of nature. Then I usually plan a few location changes so that the settings remain fresh and novel. As part of the workshop flow, these workshop areas should be close together so that I don't lose group momentum walking from place to place.

    When I sequence the activities, I choose activities for each of the four stages of Flow Learning. Depending on the group, there may be one or more activities for each stage.

    As a river flows constantly toward the sea, so the essential natural direction of Flow Learning is toward greater awareness and understanding. However, just as a river varies its mood and pace—with fast riffles, placid pools, and swirling eddies— so leaders can vary the sequence of Flow Learning's four stages. As an example, because young children have short attention spans, you may want to follow a Stage Three quiet activity with a livelier Stage One game or a calming Stage Two activity. Similarly, adults and teenagers can benefit from the change of pace that a Stage One or Two game provides.

Flow Learning is designed to be fluid and responsive. During a session, one generally moves through its basic progression (1-2-3-4), but one can also alter the sequence to address the immediate needs of the group. The leader, always closely monitoring the interest and attentiveness level, uses the activity appropriate for keeping the energy flowing happily and productively.

- Cliff: People around the world have warmly received your *nature awareness* books. What have you written since your 2014 book, *The Sky and Earth Touch Me*?

- Joseph: In June 2015, my book *Sharing Nature: Nature Awareness Activities for All Ages* was published. For this 35th anniversary edition, I completely combined and rewrote *Sharing Nature With Children and Sharing the Joy of Nature*, changing almost every sentence in both books. I expanded and enriched the Flow Learning chapters, added new activities, and included recent discoveries in science and education. This book has already been translated into the following languages: Russian, Romanian, Turkish, German, Italian, Chinese simplified and traditional, Korean, and Japanese.

- Cliff: With the increase in urbanization and digital technologies, how have they affected the need for nature education?

- Joseph: A recent Microsoft Corporation study measured how fast people's attention span has been dwindling. In the year 2000, the average Canadian's attention span was timed at twelve seconds; thirteen years later it was timed at eight seconds—a 33 percent decline. Today, even humble goldfish have a longer attention span than the average Canadian: nine seconds for the goldfish vs. eight for the Canadians.

  To be nature aware requires living in the present moment. How could it be otherwise? To see a tree demands that we actually truly see the tree. Nature activities that focus the attention on the physical senses are grounding. Nature is simple and clear; when we interact with natural environments, we can become clear and authentic ourselves.

- Cliff: If you had a magic wand, what *nature awareness* wishes do you have for students attending schools and other youth organizations?

- Joseph: Every outdoor leader *does* have a magic wand: it is nature. "I have grown taller from walking with the trees," said Karle Wilson Baker. Recent scientific studies have shown that contact with nature increases the feeling of aliveness, awe, and connectedness, and reminds us of life's higher priorities. To create a society that truly loves and reveres the natural world, we must offer its youth life-changing experiences in nature. My wish is that more leaders offer youth direct experiences of nature, where nature herself is the teacher. By bringing youth face-to-face with a stately tree, a flowery meadow, or a spring wetland, they'll begin to truly know and love the environment.

- Cliff: Thank you Joseph. You have shared the gift of your wisdom gained over many years of dedication to nature education.

> *"At times I feel as if I am spread out over the landscape and inside things, and am myself living in every tree, in the splashing of the waves, in the clouds and the animals that come and go, in the procession of the seasons. There is nothing… with which I am not linked."*
>
> —Carl G. Jung

REFERENCES

Cornell, Joseph (1979). *Sharing Nature with Children*. Nevada City, CA: Dawn Publications.

_____. (1989). Sharing the Joy of Nature: Nature activities for All Ages. Nevada City, CA: Dawn Publications.

_____. (1998). *Sharing Nature with Children*, 20th Anniversary edition, Nevada City, CA: Dawn Publications.

_____. (2000). *John Muir: My Life with Nature*. Nevada City, CA: Crystal Clarity Publishers.

_____. (2014). *The Sky and Earth Touched Me*. Nevada City, CA: Crystal Clarity Publishers.

_____. (2014). *Listening to Nature: How to Deepen Your Awareness of Nature*. Nevada City, CA: Crystal Clarity Publishers.

_____. (2015). *Sharing Nature: Nature Awareness Activities for All Ages*. Nevada City: CA: Crystal Clarity Publishers.

To find out more about Joseph Cornell's activities, visit www.sharingnature.com, www.giftofpeace.org, www.jcornell.org, and www.sky-earth.org. This interview by Clifford Knapp was adapted and updated from one published in *Thresholds in Education*, Volume XXXV, Number 3 (Fall, 2009). Pp. 45-48.

CHAPTER 5
ADVENTURE LEARNING: PERSONAL AND GROUP CHALLENGES

*"Be careful going in search of adventure—
it's ridiculously easy to find."*

—William Least Heat-Moon

Jeff McKay has been Joel's dear friend and trusted colleague for over 45 years (he is also the godfather of Joel's son, Adam). Jeff has also been one of the international pioneers in the experiential education and adventure learning fields. He has served as a Project Adventure instructor, an Outward Bound instructor, one of the early New Games lead trainers, the Wilderness Workshop co-conductor, and director of REDWOOD program at Stanford University. Jeff has also been a full-time life/leadership coach, consultant, and workshop leader for corporations, schools, and human service agencies for decades throughout North America, Latin America, Europe, and Asia. Joel brought Jeff in as a featured presenter on "From Management to Creative Leadership: Balancing Cooperation, Competition, and Challenge" at The HUMOR Project's international humor and creativity conference.

An enthusiastic and perceptive presenter, Jeff believes that play and challenge are fundamental to healing and leading. The other hat Jeff has worn (literally) is as a baseball coach—see Chapter 8 for more on that.

The following case study takes the form of an interview between Joel Goodman and Jeff McKay. Their discussion focuses on the principles and practical activities of adventure learning, as reflected in "Kids, Schools, and the School of Education," an undergraduate course he taught for years at the University of Massachusetts. Jeff paints an intriguing picture of an ongoing course that uses adventure activities in the outdoors as the medium to integrate personal learning and professional applications like teacher education. Of course, this undergraduate course could also be easily adapted for camps and K-12 school populations.

In addition to presenting many helpful principles around which to organize such a course, he also provides details about specific activities to use. In fact, as a fun challenge, you might want to see if you can do a scavenger hunt in reading this interview and track down the following activities: Playpen; Stream Trust Walk; The Wall; Swinging Log; Beam; Spin the Stick; Electric Fence; Hug Tag; and Flea Leap.

Jeff's course is a reflection of his attempts to synthesize experiential and humanistic education. Robert Frost captures his philosophy underlying the course:

It takes all sorts of in and outdoors schooling

To get adapted to my kind of fooling.

In the years that he has taught this course, Jeff has played around with many ideas. This interview provides an exciting look at the development, implementation, and evaluation of his experiential/humanistic synthesis, and challenges you to adapt and apply the principles and practice to your own situation.

- Joel: I'm wondering, Jeff, if you could give us an example of an activity that might combine humanistic and experiential learning.

- Jeff: One of the best ways for me to attempt to combine experiential and humanistic education is through the use of adventure games. These are activities that involve a group getting from point A to point B, over a wall, across a stream, or many other challenges.

  For example, we have built a Playpen at the University of Massachusetts. It's a series of posts sticking up from the ground, arranged in a circle. Some of the posts are straight up, and others come up and then fork.

  After asking people to pick a post, I define the purpose of the activity—for the group to get up on the posts. That involves some choice on the part of the participants. They need to decide which post to get on and whether to get up alone or with some assistance.

  In many cases, that kind of activity raises questions: "Why did I choose what I did?" "Did I help someone else?" "Did I need help? If so, how did I or could I have asked for help?" "How can I build cooperation in our group?"

- Joel: From what you've been saying, several things jump out at me. One is that this actively involves people, and the other is that people are given some choices. Participants are also given ways of learning from the experience by asking and answering questions. Can you give us some more details on the goals of adventure games?

- Jeff: You mentioned some of the major purposes. Active learning is the key. It involves not only participating in the task, but also "spotting"—paying attention to other people so that they don't fall and get hurt.

  It also involves participation in the sense of being aware of yourself and others. We've had people who could not physically participate for one reason or another who became involved just as much as those who were physically active.

  The whole idea of choices is important. The participant needs to make choices: whether it be which post I choose to stand on; or—if we're working in pairs—which person I choose to work with; or, how I choose to go about negotiating an obstacle. If a particular experience brings up the question of who's talking and who's listening—then it's crucial to deal with that issue, rather than with some other issue that might be on my agenda, or something that has come up in the past with a different group but may not apply in this particular case. It's important to let the discussion spring from the activity.

  The primary goal for me is to give people a chance to take a look at themselves through experience. I want them to look at how that experience and their view of themselves relate to their roles in teaching or working with others.

- Joel: You're interested in a combination of personal and professional growth for people who are considering going into teaching. I'm wondering how you came to choose humanistic education and experiential education as the two fields to synthesize.

- Jeff: A couple of things happened pretty much at the same time. One was coming to the University of Massachusetts and getting involved in a variety of ways of looking at education, particularly, the humanistic education movement. I began to see some applications for myself as a teacher and a teacher-educator. At the same time, I became involved working with Tunner Brosky, a teacher at the university who used adventure games with prospective physical education teachers.

It struck me that what I was learning in humanistic education and what I was learning with Tunner had some connections. I see humanistic education as an effective way of helping people to take a look at themselves. It seems to me that to learn about the external world and not learn about oneself is not a full education. Outdoor or experience-based education lends itself to a learn-by-doing approach.

I'm hoping that the participants in the course will get a strong experience in active learning—and also, an experience in reflecting upon and sharing their learning. I hope that if we can share those kinds of experiences as learners, then later, when many of these people go on to be teachers, they will be able to provide their students with meaningful learning experiences.

- Joel: My teachers have certainly influenced me; and their models have had an effect on the way I teach. Another goal that I'm picking up is the modeling that takes place by the facilitator of adventure games ...

Could you elaborate on how your synthesis of humanistic education and experiential education might supplement either field individually? What does the sum of the parts have that either one of the individual parts doesn't?

- Jeff: Humanistic education has been very good for me. It has been an enlightening process. However, I have found, at times, that some of my experiences with it have been lacking in reality. Sometimes, they're too nice. Perhaps only half of the picture. That's a major concern for me about humanistic education.

As far as experiential education is concerned, I think that approach to learning sometimes lacks some of the softness that humanistic education has. For example, climbing a mountain—to stress only the challenge and conquering of the mountain—may neglect some of the quieter, more reflective aspects of the experience. At times, I've found my experiences in the out-of-doors too harsh. As a result, I've felt the need to combine these approaches—to add some content and some reality to humanistic education; and to add humanistic and process approaches to outdoor experiences.

One activity many people may be familiar with is a trust or "blind" walk, which is usually associated with the humanistic movement. One of the trust experiences we do in our course is traversing a log bridge across a stream. The reality of actually crossing a stream adds something to a trust walk. It makes it a real experience. If somebody falls, the consequences are getting wet or cold. That's real, not imagined or simulated. So, that might be one example of adding the reality of outdoor experience to humanistic education.

Another example might be providing students with the challenge of getting up over a 14-foot wall. This is about as close to climbing a mountain as you can get without really climbing a mountain. I attempt to enhance the value of The Wall by helping students reflect upon and share their experience ... to ask questions and to facilitate sharing of the personal and interpersonal issues involved. That might be an example of how a humanistic process can add to outdoor experiential learning.

- Joel: You're providing "real life" experiences where there are some significant consequences. I can see how students would have an increased commitment and investment in their learning if they perceive it to be a "real life" adventure, rather than a simulation.

    What you seem to be saying is that the wall is your co-teacher. What you're doing is having the wall provide the stimulus, with you assuming the role of facilitator. You are the bridge between the stimulus and the participants by asking questions and helping students to make sense of their experience.

- Jeff: Experience as teacher ... at times I find myself losing track of that concept, but activities, such as The Wall, continue to bring me back to realizing that there's not a lot that I can teach someone. There may be many experiences that I can provide that will give students an opportunity to learn. That does allow me to be a link between the wall and the participants and to help them participate in and, to some extent, interpret and integrate that experience into their own general frame of reference.

    The wall as teacher ... that metaphor has helped me to move in some directions that feel good to me. For example, in many cases, the function of the teacher, as I see it, is first simply to present the learning experience. "Here's the wall. The task is to get the group over the wall." Secondly, I define the safety guidelines. For example, in an exercise, such as The Wall, it's important that no one hang from the top upside-down.

    Over a period of a couple of years, using these kinds of experiences as vehicles for learning, I've learned something about how to teach in a way that feels better for me. One is that, in many cases, it may not be necessary for me as teacher to define the task. In some cases, the task either defines itself or the participants can define the task.

    Last spring, we were approaching what we call the swinging log. It's about 12 feet long and hangs parallel to the ground—about a foot high. It's suspended from a couple of trees by ropes.

    I had half a dozen different tasks that I gave the group to do—get up on the log as a group, get up on the log individually, get up on the log and jump off, etc. Those had all been fine learning experiences in the past. As we walked up to the swinging log, one of the women in the group said, "Hey can we try something else?" It struck me at the moment that all I needed to do was back off and let the group define their own challenges. They came up with a number of different activities—both individual and group tasks.

    That kind of spontaneity and creativity on the part of students excites me. It's the kind of learning that really benefits me as a teacher ... I can learn from students.

    What I talked about in the example of the swinging log is the students taking responsibility for their own learning by defining the task. It's also possible, in some cases, for the students to take responsibility for how we go about the task. For example, with the wall, the normal process would be for me to define the safety guidelines, because, very clearly, the final responsibility for what happens rests on my shoulders. On the other hand, to the extent that I can involve the students in that responsibility, I think we're adding something to the course.

Another activity involves a beam that is about eight feet high. The task is for the group to get up over the beam and down to the ground on the other side.

One day, a student who had a particularly strong concern for safety and spotting said something about safety precautions. It occurred to me that this person, because of his awareness of the need for safety, might have an insight or two that he could share with the group. I asked him to express his concerns, and he came up with some really good safety guidelines. That led to other members of the group expressing concerns about safety, in general, and specific guidelines for how we negotiated the beam.

What I learned was that students, in many cases, have more going for them than we're willing to give them credit for. This particular group was quite capable of suggesting many important safety guidelines. As the one ultimately responsible, I would supplement their guidelines with any that they had missed.

The combination of students taking more responsibility for defining the learning experiences and for how we go about the learning experiences is a significant addition to the adventure approach to learning. What's exciting is that it's something I've learned from students as we have gone along.

- Joel: Such a simple concept—that the student can also be a teacher. It's encouraging to hear you talking about that actually happening. We often hear how important it is for students to take responsibility for their own learning. It often gets left at the rhetoric stage. It seems to me that the course you're involved in speaks to that very directly.

  The notion of helping people learn how to learn is something that's translated in your course by having students define tasks and by having them establish the safety guidelines. I see some direct parallels between that and what could go on in classrooms. There's no reason why students couldn't have a part in establishing some of the classroom rules or guidelines—just as they can establish safety guidelines in an adventure learning course.

  Another basic principle is that it doesn't make sense to cram a lot of information into students—especially before they've even asked the question. Your course seems to help students create and participate in their own learning. They're the ones asking the questions, and out of that comes some motivation and interest in whatever it is they're going to learn.

- Jeff: The phrase you used—that the student can also be a teacher—really gets at what education can be about. Teaching and learning are not processes that can be separated into two discrete roles. For those who are going to be teachers, their experience as learners needs to include some experience in "teaching"—taking responsibility for what and how they learn.

  The second phrase you mentioned that speaks to me is "learning how to learn." That's what it's all about. The kinds of skills that we, as teachers, need to provide for students are skills in problem-solving, and communication—the lifetime skills that are not only learning how to learn, but learning how to live. Those are not necessarily teachable in the traditional sense. They are, however, learnable.

- Joel: The motto for your course, from what I've been picking up, could be "learning how to learn, learning how to live, learning how to teach." It seems to me the course encourages participants to take a look at themselves and their learning styles. It seems the course is also a vehicle for helping them take a look at issues relating to teaching. Could you give an example of a typical class meeting?

- Jeff: Yes. In any class meeting, it's important at the beginning to have some kind of experience, which reestablishes our learning community. For example, we might play a game called Hug Tag. Someone is "it," and everybody else tries to stay away from "it" by hugging each other. If you're hugging somebody, you're safe, but if you're moving from one person to another, and you're alone, then you may get caught.

    We also do an individual challenge in most classes—for example, jumping from one platform to another. We call that the Flea Leap. Each individual "measures" the degree of risk—(for example, "Do I jump from the front or the back of the upper platform?") and then acts on that choice.

Anna Dudko/Hemera/Thinkstock

We also do an experience in a small group or in parts, such as a variety of Trust Walks. And then finally, some kind of all-group task that involves problem-solving and initiative, such as getting over the wall.

- Joel: Are there any other common threads that run through either a particular class or the entire course itself? Are there any "rituals" or traditions that you incorporate or that seem to emerge from the students?
- Jeff: There are a variety of supplementary learning experiences, such as personal journals, a group log, readings, out-of-class experiences, and a major activity project. The purpose of all those parts is to integrate our experience in the course with some writing, reading, and outside experience. For example, I ask students to keep a journal about their experiences each week. I'm interested in their actions, reactions, thoughts, and feelings. And, to a lesser extent, their observations of what went on in the group as a whole.

  The group log is different. Each week, one member of the group writes in a public group log. At the start of the next class, he reads his entry. I'm trying to promote an understanding that any individual's impression of what happened is true. If one person perceives an activity as X and another perceives an activity as Y, that's fine. The message is that each person's perspective is valid.

  Each week, I read (and I encourage students to read) a quotation or two that relates to our experience. For example, "If I give you a fish, you eat tonight. If I teach you to fish, you eat forever." The students enjoy the quotations, which often provide food for thought or a conceptual handle on our experience.
- Joel: The group log seems to get at another of your principles: trying to get students out of the "right answer" syndrome.
- Jeff: The right answer syndrome is a classic example of something worth unlearning. It comes up sooner or later, and in the middle, too. I've been asked many times: "How have other groups done this?" or "What's the best way to do it?" I do not answer that question directly, but respond, "What do you see as other ways of going about this task?" Occasionally, we'll do the same activity two different times in two different ways to help us see that there is no right answer. Gradually, students become more comfortable with finding or creating a solution, and not necessarily "the answer."
- Joel: So, there's more than one way to "skin the wall." That obviously has some implications for teaching, by helping people to expand their repertoire of teaching skills, and not getting stuck in the rut of "here's the right way or only way to teach a certain subject." You've mentioned another medium to get across your message: assignments.
- Jeff: One of the assignments we do is to spend some time with children outside of the classroom (e.g., ride the bus to and from school, attend recess, or eat lunch with children). My intent is to get students to look at learning a little, but out of the normal set or typical school environment. The other assignments are similar in that they are experiential (e.g., interviewing a student-teacher, attending a PTA meeting).

  Finally, each student participates in a major activity project—volunteering at a hospital, serving as an assistant scoutmaster, working as a teacher's aide, etc. Once again, I hope the student will learn about education through actual involvement.

  It's important that the student find his own activity project, rather than for me to set up an activity project for him. I give him some guidelines and possibilities, but it's his choice and responsibility. For some students, that freedom of choice is difficult.

- Joel: I would call that helping students to move from the "choose-one-of-the-above" syndrome to "choose-one-or-none-of-the-above-and-create-your own."
- Jeff: It goes back to the concept of unlearning. Let me talk about unlearning as it relates to these parts of the course. For example, I'm aware that a weekly journal can become more of a "requirement" than a vehicle for learning. So, I say: "At least once during the course, the log is going to be a burden, rather than a learning experience; so don't do it." This surprises students a little. As I see it, not doing it is more valuable than doing it in that particular case.

     I tell students that throwing a reading in the wastebasket is clearly irresponsible. On the other hand, reading it cover-to-cover because I gave it to them, or because it's a requirement of the course, is also irresponsible. So, I ask them to start the reading and find out if it has any meaning for them. Also, to be aware if they're reading it for me or for the course. If they are reading it for me or the course, then they need to be aware of that and either work through it or lay the reading aside for a while. If, upon returning to the reading, the student still finds himself reading it for external reasons, it may be a learning experience for him not to read it.

     I'm also interested in having students make some decisions regarding assignments. I say that if spending time with children on a bus or at lunch or recess doesn't have any personal meaning, then it's important to create an alternative learning experience. Over a period of time, students start acting on those kinds of options, and that's exciting.
- Joel: I personally agree with this approach. I can also imagine some teachers saying, "Hey, what are you doing? Are you saying that the assignments you give aren't important? Are you taking away the authority of the teacher using the assignment as a 'vehicle for motivation'?"
- Jeff: One of the teachers who voices those kinds of concerns is me. It's very difficult for me, at times, to give students that kind of freedom. It raises the question, "Who's in charge here?" I recognize that. It is presumptuous to assume that, because something has meaning for me, it will have meaning for my students.

     I don't see myself giving students the option to do nothing. I'm giving them the choice to do a, b, c, or a more meaningful experience of their own design. I ask them to check out that option with me if they have any questions or reservations about it.
- Joel: You've given many details about the course components. Could you give a broader view of the 15-week course as a whole? How do you know what to put when and where and after what and for whom?
- Jeff: For the first month of the course, we participate in a variety of experiences. I do not place much emphasis on educational issues. Rather, I'm attempting to allow students the opportunity to experience many different learning activities and to talk about them. To the extent that those experiences raise issues, we deal with them.
- Joel: What you're seeking to do at first is to get people actively involved and avoid intellectual head-tripping.
- Jeff: Yes, I think that's necessary. As I've mentioned, one concern I do emphasize, early in the course, is the concept of unlearning. For example, just recently in one

of the classes, we were talking about different ways of learning. I said that one way to present adventure games would be for me to define the task, demonstrate or tell them how to solve the task, and then say, "OK, now go to it." One of the participants responded, "Yes, I know what you're saying, but if you had pulled that on us the first day, I don't think you'd have had any argument, because that's been our school experience."

That strikes me as a good example of why the concept and process of unlearning is necessary. As a teacher, I can unlearn a lot of my tendencies to tell students how to do it; and similarly, they can unlearn a lot of their experience that has said, "Teacher, tell us how to do it."

- Joel: It appears that one of your major goals in the first part of the course is to have students change their "set"—not only of their role as students and the method in which learning is going to take place, but also of the role of the teacher. What you're trying to do is break them of the learning-by-rote method. You're trying to build in readiness, so that when you try a new approach, they're not going to tell you to "hit the rote" or ask you for the answers.

- Jeff: I can give an example of altering our normal set of assumptions about teaching/learning. One of the activities we do that is an experience in unlearning is called Spin the Stick. The student takes a stick about a yard long and holds it up over her head. She stands straight—arms over her head—with the stick pointing to the sky. When she has spun around 10 times, she simply lays the stick in front of her and tries to step over it. At least nine times out of 10, the student falls to the ground, laughing …

There are different ways of looking at that experience. One is that there's no point to it at all. On that level, that's exactly the point. The experience speaks for itself. It's fun. On another level, the point is that Spin the Stick is an exercise in failure.

As an introduction to the course, the message is—"it's okay to do something that either has no point at all, or if it has a point, it's that it's fun, or it's acceptable to take a chance and to fall on your rear-end." Failure is okay. You have what John Holt calls the freedom to fail and what Carl Rogers calls the freedom to learn.

It's important that the student has the opportunity to try some new experiences and to risk to some extent. If it doesn't work, that's all right. That's a way of unlearning.

- Joel: It seems that the "fear of failure" is something that needs to be addressed— especially if you're talking about the kinds of physical challenges that are involved in adventure education. In the process of breaking set or unlearning, people are risking extending their limits. You say that the first month of a semester-long course might be involved with experiencing or unlearning. How do you follow that up?

- Jeff: In the second month of the course, we begin to take a look at what we're doing and how it relates to the learning process. I'm hoping that—after learning how to unlearn, we can learn how to learn.

Let me see if I can give you an example. All different kinds of issues come up in the process of a group getting over the eight-foot-high beam. In most cases, the group will explore alternatives. This is an aspect of learning—the process of problem solving and making decisions.

In deciding how they're going to get over the beam, the issues of communication may come up. Who's talking? Who's listening? To what extent am I listening to what you have to say? To what extent am I trying to make sure that it gets done my way?

The task raises another issue—leadership and followership. Who is exercising leadership? To what extent can one move from leading to stepping back and following?

Those kinds of issues come up again and again. What I'm trying to do is to facilitate learning from their immediate experience.

- Joel: It seems clear to me that the two components—the experiential (doing) and the humanistic (learning from doing)—come together in this phase of the course: the experiential (the task of getting over the wall or beam) and the humanistic (the process of helping students to make sense of the experience). How about another example of a specific activity that would combine doing and learning from doing?

- Jeff: In the Electric Fence, we string a rope about five feet off the ground and give the group an eight-foot pole. After identifying essential safety and spotting guidelines, we ask them to get from one side of the rope to the other, using only the pole, without touching the "electric fence."

Once again, it's hard to guess what will happen, because it's almost a guarantee that, if I predict that X will happen, then Y will happen. In general, however, the group needs to choose among alternatives.

It's interesting to observe how what happens, happens. I need to refrain from giving my observations to the students and instead try to facilitate their awareness of the process of how they went about what they did. After the experience, I attempt to facilitate the discussion first on a factual level. "What happened?" "What did you do?" Then to the extent that it flows, I attempt to move the discussion toward personal values and feelings raised by the experience. Then I move to the question of learning—how does this relate to solving a problem and the process of learning in general?

- Joel: Can you recall some of the statements that students have made in the past in response to "What has this got to do with learning?"

- Jeff: I think there are some generalizations that can be made. Obviously, everyone's experience of an activity like the Electric Fence is different, and that's what makes it exciting. What's interesting is that after a month or so, students start to perceive the need for working together, the need for trust and support among the participants, and the realization that leadership includes followership. Their awareness of these kinds of teaching-learning concepts develops gradually through experience.

- Joel: One thing that stands out from the Electric Fence is that cooperation is built into the task. The task is defined so that the entire group has to get over the fence if they are to succeed. Do you consciously focus on cooperative tasks?

Another way of structuring that task would be to say: "Every person for themselves." Everybody over the fence as best you can." It seems to me the task—whether it be the Electric Fence or The Wall—is designed with a cooperative element. Do students ever say, "Hey, this isn't life. Life is competition."

- Jeff: That's a significant question. Yes, many of the experiences are defined as group tasks. We do attempt to address the question of competition and survival of the fittest, because that certainly is a reality in our educational system and in our society.

  For example, one of the games I use has two parts. The first part is called Stand Off. Two people stand about arm's length apart and try to knock each other off balance by hitting hands. That is a challenging game and also a competitive game, as it is basically you against me.

  Then we move from Stand Off to a different version of the game called Human Spring. The same people, rather than trying to knock each other off balance, extend their arms forward and push off their hands as they spring forward and then backward. It's still a challenge, but now it becomes more of a cooperative effort, because the goal is to help each other maintain balance after springing off one another. We spend some time talking about Stand Off and Human Spring, and how "challenge" is a common thread in both games.

- Joel: I'm intrigued with the notion of challenge being the bridge between cooperation and competition. How do you move from having students learning about learning in the second part of the course to learning about teaching in the third part?

- Jeff: It happens in a variety of ways. Over the period of a few months, my function as a teacher, the wall's function as teacher, and the students' role as learner/ teacher have a cumulative effect on the students' awareness of "teaching."

  Another way that's more structured is to facilitate a discussion distilling the common elements of teaching/learning inherent in the activities. We talk about problem-solving, cooperation, leadership-followership, communication, and related concepts. I ask them to speak about their experience as learners in adventure games, so that we keep the process tied to real happenings. I also ask them to reflect upon and share their experience of me as a teacher.

  The next step, and the most difficult one, is: "What are the elements of adventure learning that pertain to learning in general?" In many cases, it's possible to incorporate some of the elements of adventure learning into a more traditional environment—in elementary or secondary classrooms.

- Joel: What you're doing is using your experiences in this course as the subject matter—as the textbook, in a sense, as they investigate teaching. It seems that the third part of the course invites them to read "the book" within themselves (helping them to develop self-literacy skills). They come up with their own answers to defuzz "teaching," and draw some implications as future teachers.

- Jeff: Yes, I think the key word is "implication." Over a period of time, those implications become more explicit. These awarenesses become more conscious through reflecting on what's going on and sharing with other members of the group and me.

Beyond the implications are the applications. "How does this approach to learning apply to you as someone who's interested in teaching?" "How can you incorporate cooperation into learning experiences you design for students?" "How can you provide learning experiences that ask students to define and solve problems so that the learning is real?"

- Joel: You mentioned some specific questions that you might ask. I can see where students could make some direct ties between the experience and the implications and applications to teaching. What are some specific activities at this stage of the course?

- Jeff: In the final phase of the course, we do some classroom-type experiences that spring from our outdoor experiences. For example, if we're going to learn about different teaching styles, I present a lesson in different ways, and then ask them which method they preferred and why. Rather than telling about different approaches to learning, I allow them to experience those different approaches.

  Another example is an activity that's similar to a scavenger hunt. It's called a School Search, in which the students learn about a school by exploring. I might ask a question such as, "What indications are there that the librarian is attempting to motivate children to read?" The intent is to have the students search that out and then take a look at the educational issues involved.

  Another example might be to have students interview a student teacher. Certainly, it would be possible for me to tell them about student teaching. However, they probably would learn more by talking with someone who is presently in that role. In some cases, that requires students to risk—not climbing over the wall—but to risk contacting someone they don't know and interviewing that person to find out about student teaching.

  I try to do a variety of indoor, nonphysical activities that incorporate at least some of the elements of adventure learning. Hopefully, my students make the transfer from adventure games to classroom teaching.

- Joel: The sequencing in your course seems to get at a couple of things. One is that people are involved in and responsible for their own learning. Second, what you're doing is providing many different vehicles for students to get that direct experience, which will be meaningful to them.

- Jeff: I think that's a middle ground between teacher-directed, mandatory learning and no learning at all.

- Joel: What you're talking about here is "structured freedom." It's not an authoritarian situation, in which there is order but no freedom. It's not a laissez-faire situation, where there's freedom but no order.

- Jeff: Sure, I think there are a variety of alternatives between structure and freedom. For example, in another assignment, I might say: "Part one—this is required—part two—pick a, b, or c—part three—design your own."

- Joel: I'm curious about evaluation of these kinds of experiences. What are some of the principles or beliefs you have about evaluation?

- Jeff: Evaluation is a difficult question for me. I believe in process evaluation, because I don't think it's possible to quantify somebody's learning. My primary concern is that evaluation spring directly from experience, rather than disrupt the flow of learning. I use evaluation to improve the course and get more student input.
- Joel: So, what you're talking about is focusing on improving, as opposed to proving.
- Jeff: For my purposes, the best kind of evaluation is self-evaluation. I ask students to look back at their commitment to and participation in the course, and to look forward to their next steps. I also ask them to evaluate me as a teacher and the course as a learning experience.
- Joel: So the focus on evaluation is in terms of a "review, a view, and a preview." Having students review what has gone on for them, take a look at themselves now, and then preview what's coming up.

    I've picked up two ways that you gather evaluation data. One is directly asking questions. The second is the group log.
- Jeff: The log gives me a great deal of information about how and where to go the next week. For example, a student recently wrote about an activity, "I really thought the activity was too easy." So, the next week, we did some more challenging activities, which the students really enjoyed. The journals and the group log often help me in my planning.
- Joel: It's interesting that you legitimize students telling you "where to go." I imagine many people might be a little wary of that. You seem to take the data they provide you and use it in making decisions.

    Using some of those tools that you've described, I'm wondering what kinds of information you've picked up from students. Can you give us some examples of what they report?
- Jeff: Some of the experiences we do are very difficult physically and, at first glance, they look like they might even be impossible. Students say things like, "Oh, we'll never be able to do that." Or, "I can't do that." Over a period of time, whatever it takes them to accomplish the task, they get the message that "I can't do it" is all in their heads. The experience of "doing it" helps students to feel their own power and skill and to learn from their successes.

    When students negotiate a problem, that's a really strong learning experience for them. I can remember one woman last spring, who looked at the 14-foot wall the first day and was scared. She said, "There's just no way I'm going to be able to do that. I don't know whether the group's going to be able to get over the wall—but not me."

    A few months later, with a great deal of struggle, I think she had really learned from this accomplishment. A large part of the course is focused around activities that have success built into them in one form or another. There's certainly room for failure in the course, and I think it's important, upon occasion. In most cases, however, individuals and the group, as a whole, have some success.
- Joel: What I'm picking up is that, in addition to learning by doing, you're also building opportunities for succeeding by doing. The act of courage at confronting that wall

is something that can be encouraging. It seems like some of these experiences, in a supportive, cooperative atmosphere could lead people to feel better about themselves. They might come out of a course like this with an attitude of "I think I can do it."

- Jeff: There's a lot of truth in that. I think the key is that success is real, and it's obvious. If the wall's there, and you start on one side and you end up on the other, all you've got to do is knock on wood to realize that you have accomplished something.
- Joel: What you have throughout the course is a built-in evaluation mechanism for the students. They get data: I either got over the wall or I didn't. At the same time, the wall for me is a metaphor for other walls that we encounter and can overcome in our lives.
- Jeff: Let me conclude with some words from the students themselves—I think it's appropriate that they "get in the last word."

> "I am immediately aware that I have unlearned a certain amount of the formalness of my previous education—at least enough to allow some self-directed learning and free expression."

> "I used to think I learned when I did well on a test. Then learning seemed to be listening to what the teacher had to say. I think right now learning is being able to apply information to my life. Learning is living …"

DÉJÀ VU: WHAT'S NEW?: LOOKING BACK, MOVING FORWARD

In preparing the updated edition of this book years later, Joel and Jeff pick up and continue their conversation.

- Joel: In our earlier interview, you quoted Robert Frost. I know that he has been a favorite of yours—you have drawn many insights from his words. Do you have a new Frost poem as a teacher for you?
- Jeff: "We dance around a ring and suppose, but the secret sits in the center and knows." My take on Frost's couplet is that we need to get out of our supposing heads and get into our knowing bodies.
- Joel: What are some suppositions you have been playing with over the years?
- Jeff: If we are trying to empower students through adventure learning, we need to consider when to tell and when to ask. For example, as you and I talked about earlier, we certainly need to clearly get across the safety guidelines for a challenging activity. Perhaps we can ask them for the safety guidelines first, and then only add anything that they may have missed, or repeat what they have offered. This might give them the opportunity to take responsibility for their own safety as a significant aspect of their learning. And, if they think it was their idea, they are more likely to pay attention to it! Safety first. But, maybe their responsible version of safety.
- Joel: I can safely say that one of the ideas that you emphasized in our first conversation was that of unlearning.

- Jeff: What I am learning about unlearning is that it's hard. Our habits seem to be deeply ingrained in the body and mind. To unlearn them, we first need to recognize them. Let's call that "awareness." The awareness then gives us the opportunity for choice—that is, the choice to practice a new habit. Suffice it to say that learning needs to be preceded by unlearning. And by learning, I mean something we can take action on, as opposed to just something we have learned in the head only.

- Joel: What have you unlearned and learned about leadership?

- Jeff: What I have learned over the years, and what I am in the process of relearning now, is that the key to leadership is self-leadership. Not the leadership of others, but the leadership of self. My experience is that when I manage myself well, I manage others well. And when I don't, I don't. Period.

    We need to help students learn more than self-literacy. We need to help students learn self-management. Adventure learning activities, presented in an empowering way, can provide the grist for the mill for such learning. Participants can learn about leadership—and their own leadership—through the activities and follow-up processing conversations.

- Joel: You and I had also talked about the structure-freedom continuum in teaching and in living. Have any new light bulbs gone on for you on that?

- Jeff: One of the best expressions about learning that I have seen was a button that said, "Structure Freedom." I continue to learn that we educators are rarely right on the money. Either we are too far into structure (rigidity), or we are too far into freedom (chaos). It seems that the key again is awareness—awareness of self. If we can recognize that we are too far in one direction or the other, we can center ourselves and re-balance. And maybe model for students how to do the same.

    As a former Outward Bound instructor, I am learning—at my ripe old age—that the game becomes Inward Bound. Outward and Inward. Outer and Inner. Onward!!!

- Joel: Jeff, thanks for yet another Onward and Upward Bound conversation.

> *"The biggest adventure you can take*
> *is to live the life of your dreams."*
>
> —Oprah Winfrey

CHAPTER 6

LOOKING BACK AND LOOKING AGAIN: REFLECTING AND REVIEWING

"Experience is not what happens to you. It is what you do with what happens to you."

—Aldous Huxley

Many outdoor leaders want to know more about how to help participants get the most meaning out of their experiences and transfer this learning to their lives back home. One way to do this is through leading reflecting (looking back) or reviewing (looking again) sessions with participants during or following their activities.

One of the authors (Cliff Knapp) was fortunate to meet one of the most qualified facilitators of reflecting/reviewing in the world on a trip to Scotland. Roger Greenaway from Stirling, Scotland hosted him for two days, several years ago. Both individuals have a strong interest in this aspect of experiential learning, so they had a lot to share. Roger, who stays in top physical condition by windsurfing and ultrarunning, took Cliff for a brisk walk to the top of a hill, and along the way they talked about their educational philosophies. The following interview captures some of Roger's views on facilitating outdoor learning.

Roger is a prolific writer and energetic workshop leader specializing in making experience-based learning more participatory, dynamic, and effective. His most recent book is titled, *Active Reviewing*, and one of his latest articles is "Six of the Best Ways of Introducing Active Reviewing." He and Cliff recently co-authored a chapter on this topic in the *Routledge International Handbook of Outdoor Studies.*

Roger is widely sought after and travels the world because of his dedication to this topic and his enthusiastic energy when leading training sessions. Over the past 20 years, he has led workshops and consulted in 35 countries. His doctoral dissertation was a study of powerful learning experiences in management learning outdoors. He has been a teacher of English and outdoor education for many years, and was first exposed to this idea of reflecting and reviewing when he worked at Brathay, a development training center in England. After writing several handbooks on this topic, he launched his career of leading active and creative reviewing workshops in the 1990s. His website, http://reviewing.co.uk, provides a rich source of information about his favorite topic. Hopefully, you will catch some of Roger's fascination and excitement for reflecting and reviewing in this interview.

- Cliff: What does experiential learning or learning through experience mean to you?
- Roger: I see learning through experience as a respectful and personal approach to learning; paying attention to experience means paying attention to the "experiencer." It is learners who have the most direct access to the experiential data from which they can learn.

  Compared to more institutionalized and traditional forms of learning, I see experiential learning as more active, more responsible, more holistic, more real, and more open to interpretation. In experiential learning, the data are not pre-constructed or pre-packaged and ready for learners to digest. The data are out there either in the physical and social environment or within the learner. Often, it is produced dynamically, as these different sources interact. Learners need to notice, read, and interpret the data to make sense of it and draw their own conclusions.

The teacher/leader/facilitator is not essential for experiential learning to take place, but can have a vitally important role in helping participants develop the confidence and skills for learning effectively from experience. This role might include either challenging the conclusions or challenging the process by which these conclusions were reached.

Being an effective experiential learner encompasses a very different set of skills compared to those of being an effective indoor classroom student. Once these skills are learned, they can be applied to all kinds of life experiences. The most powerful learning of all is learning to become a better experiential learner.

- Cliff: The experiential/adventure literature reveals that several different terms are used to describe the process of facilitating meaningful learning, including the following: teaching for transfer, reviewing, reflecting, debriefing, and processing. How do you use these terms?

- Roger: During a program, the leader will be facilitating learning from experience. After the program is over, it is usually up to students to choose whether and how they will transfer what they have learned. By this time, the leader/facilitator may no longer be around to support the process of transfer. Transfer seems to be an unsupported process that depends on student motivation. I am not suggesting that this is best practice. I am simply explaining my understanding of the term "transfer"—it tends to be learner-driven and unfacilitated.

  Concerning the terms reviewing, reflecting, debriefing, and processing, I think some of these terms describe what the facilitator is doing, and others describe what the learner is doing. "Reflecting" is what the learner does, and "debriefing" is what the facilitator does. The other two terms "reviewing" and "processing" apply to actions of either facilitators or learners, especially to group processes. For example, the leader might say, "Let's review what was happening at the point where you felt that the teamwork really improved." In my world, "reflecting" usually applies to personal experience, while "reviewing" usually applies to group experience. But none of this is very tidy or exact, and usage really comes down to personal or cultural preference—or on how closely you want to keep to John Dewey's terms— "experience," "reflection," and "learning."

- Cliff: When you facilitate groups to help them learn from their outdoor experiences, what are some factors you consider to help them bring more lasting meaning to the activities?

- Roger: I think "variety" comes to the top of my list. Many good things can happen when sitting in a circle, but circles are by no means the only social setting for making meaning from activities. It is important to mix in personal thinking time (such as finding a natural object that has personal significance) together with reflective/creative tasks in groups of twos or threes, and then, when coming together as whole group, using a variety of reviewing activities in addition to talking in a circle.

  This variety is partly to influence interest and energy. It is partly to ensure that there is usually something for each person to do (other than sit and listen).

And it is partly to create effective learning pathways through these reflective processes. There are at least as many good learning pathways as there are ways to have good conversations.

To bring about lasting meaning, we need to be alive to the nature of the learning experience. A moment of high confidence can last longer if the people are invited to relive key moments through action replay. This factor is a way of acknowledging and celebrating that moment and of sharing the story with others. Replays can help key experiences to live on in future experiences (an echo of John Dewey's words). Replays also help to keep learning in the physical realm. This aspect is helpful if there is a risk that abstract learning might float away from the vivid source that gave rise to the original learning.

Various kinds of artwork, including environmental art and photography, can also assist with both initial learning and lasting meaning. Keeping curiosity alive by treating learners as explorers or adventurers can help with the kinds of learning that build up over time. That concept needs to be continually re-examined. This factor can be true for complex, mind-boggling subjects, as well as for continuing development as a person or as a leader. These are never-ending projects that require continuing curiosity, experimenting, and learning.

- Cliff: I've discovered that many teacher/leaders do not practice reviewing/reflecting strategies as often as needed for meaningful learning to occur. If you agree, why do you think this is so?
- Roger: As a fan of reviewing, my agreement is almost automatic. I think the reasons why people neglect reviewing are many. Sometimes it is to maximize the time outside for the active outdoor experience. That's where the main energy and interest are and that is usually the main reason for going outdoors. Maybe there is a fear that reviewing will drain interest and energy, and a belief that reflection can be saved for later, when back indoors (bye-bye to the teachable moment!). Maybe there's a lack of appreciation of the amazing places and opportunities for reflection and review when outdoors. Maybe the intention is to "teach by experience" with most of the knowledge input supplied by the "teacher as teller." This is a different paradigm in which reflection adds little value. Maybe the leaders want the whole experience to be as different as possible from the normal classroom, and they fear that reviewing could make things too much like formal schooling. Maybe there is also a lack of appreciation of the many ways in which reviewing can work better outside and can be very different from a typical classroom experience. Maybe there is a lingering belief in the idea that "mountains speak for themselves"—or that "well designed activities speak for themselves." They don't! And even if they did—how would we know what each individual is hearing, feeling, and concluding?

  We have a responsibility to find out what these echo chambers of the mind are saying to participants by asking if everyone is getting value from their experiences. We can also learn about the effectiveness of our facilitation if we stop to listen to participants' interpretations of these echoes.

I think we have a wider responsibility to help participants become better experiential learners. To do this, they need to get in the habit of reflecting on their experiences, expressing what they have experienced or learned, and showing interest in the experiences and views of others. There might be some rare exceptions where participants simply wish to savor the experience. "Pure experience" can meet important developmental needs, but I do not see how meaningful learning can be achieved without the inclusion of a reflective process.

- Cliff: What conditions or climate do you attempt to create as you build a sense of community through reviewing/reflection sessions?

- Roger: I usually avoid classic group-building games in which the leader calls all the tunes and there is high pressure for full participation right from the start. Such games can inadvertently set precedents for unthinking obedience and for automatically conforming to group norms. This situation can make it difficult or confusing if the leader later wants to encourage questioning authority, provoking curiosity, accepting diverse views, thinking creatively or critically, taking risks, developing self-confidence, encouraging choice, respecting individual differences, or avoiding "groupthink."

My preference is to start at the very outset with activities that respect and explore group diversity by showing an interest in the range of different experiences, perspectives, and ideas. This step can readily be achieved when reviewing an observation walk by asking, "What did you notice?" or "What interested you most?" I generally want to create a community in which all individuals are listened to and respected and feel that they have something valuable to contribute. So, it is helpful for leaders to use a variety of engaging reviewing methods that create excellent opportunities for everyone to listen, show respect, and contribute.

- Cliff: How do you decide when to intervene by leading a structured activity and when to refrain from intervening into the ongoing group process?

- Roger: I am not sure if you mean intervening in an open discussion with a more structured review process, or if you mean intervening during a structured activity with some kind of on-the-spot review. Either way, these are difficult judgments to make, because with any leader intervention, there is an upside and a downside. For example, you will clearly want to intervene, if there is a safety issue. But, even then, you can intervene without taking over completely, by saying something like, "Wait! I think you should do one last safety check." The downside is that the more you intervene, the more you risk taking away responsibilities and opportunities for learning through experience. The upside is that there are many ways of intervening that can enhance responsibilities and opportunities if you come up with a suitably designed reviewing method that includes special responsibilities within it.

As a general rule, the main purpose of an intervention is to keep participants actively engaged in the experiential learning processes whether they are experiencing, reflecting, analyzing, experimenting, or supporting others in such processes. Interventions that are too "helpful" or too controlling risk closing down these experiential learning processes. The likely result is that the main learning paradigm flips back into a more "teacherly" one. Reversing the flip back into experiential learning is the more difficult direction, because, in most cases, classroom teaching and learning is everyone's default mode or even their "comfort zone."

- Cliff: What have you learned about facilitating "powerful learning experiences" and transfer of learning to "the real world" back home?

- Roger: Powerful learning happens in many ways. It is important to be alert to possibilities, as well as to the different ways in which each individual is experiencing, responding, and learning. But if we mostly work through groups rather than through a series of one-to-one conversations, then we need to create groups that support a variety of different pathways. If you are working with a group that will be together after the event, it is important that they have a suitable follow-up project for which they take full or substantial responsibility. If the group comes from different places, then it is helpful to set up some kind of co-coaching or support system. And if participants are in the habit of checking their mobile devices, then it would be wise to have a transfer strategy that exploits the use of these devices.

On one hand, you might find that you have created an excellent transfer strategy, but that the program has not truly ignited their interest. On the other hand, you might find you have really ignited their interest through an excellent program, but they are at a loss for what they can do about it, because you have little to offer to support transfer. I would generally support designing for transfer long before the program has started.

In most programs, the transfer strategy would include ensuring that participants have many opportunities for making choices and decisions, and acting on them within the program. At the point that the program ends, participants will already be in the habit of choosing, deciding, and acting, and will have developed their confidence in being "creators" rather than "consumers." If programs generally treat participants as obedient consumers who are led all the way through the program, do not expect them to suddenly become proactive "creators" after the program ends in what is usually a much less supportive environment.

- Cliff: Thanks Roger. Your words will help those who wonder how to help their participants get the most out of experiential learning.

"What is of greatest consequence in a person's life is not just the nature and extent of his or her experiences, but what has been learned from them."

—Norman Cousins

REFERENCES

Greenaway, R., Bogdan, V. & Iepure, C. (2015). *Active reviewing: A practical guide for trainers and facilitators.* Charleston, SC: Bogdan Vaida.

Greenaway, R. & Knapp, C. E. (2016). *Routledge international handbook of outdoor studies*, "Reviewing and Reflection: Connecting People to Experiences," pp. 260-268. In Humberstone, B., Prince, H. & Henderson, K. A. (Eds.). London/New York: Routledge Taylor & Francis Group.

CHAPTER 7
PLAYFAIR: EVERYBODY'S GUIDE TO NONCOMPETITIVE GAMES

"People are more fun than anybody."

—Dorothy Parker

Matt Weinstein and Joel Goodman go back a long ways—over 45 years, in fact. They met in graduate school and became fast friends fast. They went on to co-author the groundbreaking book in the field of cooperative play, *Playfair: Everybody's Guide to Noncompetitive Play*. Early on, Joel had the good fortune to tour colleges putting on Playfairs for hundreds of college students during freshman-orientation programs, which gave him even more appreciation and respect for Matt and Pamela Kekich's groundbreaking work (and play).

There has been a growing need and awareness in this country of the importance of helping people learn how to spend their leisure time. There has also been a concomitant interest in exploring noncompetitive, win-win forms of play and recreation.

In 1975, Matt Weinstein and Pamela Kekich began to offer Playfair events around the country. Each Playfair is a unique blend of noncompetitive play experiences, audience-participation comedy, and newly-created group challenges. Groups from 10 to 10,000 have found Playfair to be an enjoyable way to focus on the nature and nurture of "play" … in essence, helping people to create their own recreation in a constructive and cooperative mode.

In the following conversation with Joel Goodman, Matt and Pamela offer insights on how to make games less competitive, less exclusive, and less demeaning—and how to build cooperation, inclusion, and self-esteem into the larger "game of life." They also describe a number of organizing principles for the Playfairs, as well as a variety of specific games they have created. You might be on the lookout for games with such intriguing titles as Three-Way Tug-of-War; Imaginary Tug-of-War; Big Ball Games; Blob Tag; Touch Blue; Incorporations; Big Wind Blows; Three Positions; Introductions; Elbow Fruit Hop; Off-Balance; Human Spring; Morra; and Wonderful Circle. On your mark, get set, go play!

- Joel: Here's a very simple question to start: How did you ever get interested in doing what you're doing?
- Pamela: When I started teaching and doing my master's in elementary education, it seemed like there was a point when children changed the way they played with one another and began to acquire physical inhibitions. So, I started to look at "play." There are lots of books about organized sports, but not many about play. I found out that there is a change in the way children play with each other about the age of four or five. Then, by the time they are six or seven, they already have learned the way we all know to play—through organized games that are competitive, uncreative, nonimaginative, and not physically playful. Before that, we all went through a stage of being inventive and fantasizing our experiences.
- Joel: You made a distinction between play and sports. Can you say more about that?
- Pamela: That's an important question. Play does not necessarily involve rules that are set, and it is not necessarily organized. The way we played as young children was mostly by making things up and creating situations. In more organized sports, the rules are set. The acting out of those rules is more important than the creating of them.
- Joel: Matt, how did you get interested in "play"?

- Matt: I started working with games when I was training teachers in creative dramatics and theatre. What I became interested in was letting people have that experience of improvisation, of creating something together—but without so much of the stress on pantomime skills.

  When Pamela and I got together, we thought that we could give people wonderful group experiences of a kind that no one has done—that concentrate on positive, exuberant feelings through playing with people. We had a feeling that that was a good direction to take. However, what we found is that the traditional games that everybody plays were not going to work for our purposes. They actually inhibited the playfulness in a lot of ways by setting people against each other, or by setting up competitive win-lose and "I feel-good-when-you-feel-bad" situations.

  We did not want to abandon our idea that people could play together, and have a unique, positive experience. So, what we did was to abandon almost all of the games we knew as children—changed them around and invented new games that worked for our purposes.

- Joel: So, your purpose in play is not to have one group of people feeling badly and one group feeling good? The kind of play you're talking about doesn't have to happen.

- Matt: Right, we avoid setting up direct confrontations like that. In our Playfairs, we used to have spoofs on that competitive feeling by having a tug-of-war. We employed a three-way tug-of-war, using two ropes tied together so that there are three ends. It is very unlikely that one team could win against the combined forces of the other two teams. So, we do play around with those traditions, so that people can get a humorous look at them. For example, you might also have a two-team tug-of-war with an imaginary rope. The teams take their cues from a leader who directs the action and determines who is winning.

- Joel: There are a lot of adults and young people today who are saying, "Hey, competition is great—in the kind of world in which we live, you need to learn how to compete." What kind of response do you have to people who ask, "Why do we need this cooperative form of play?"

- Matt: I think what you just said is true. But it's only true if you limit your vision to saying that's the way the world is, and it'll never change. We think that it can change, and that the world doesn't always have to be like that. We are taking a small step to show people that there are other ways to interact. Hopefully, people will take this philosophy from the playing field and see that it is possible to live lovingly and cooperatively.

- Pamela: People get lots of opportunities to find out what's wrong with themselves, but not many opportunities to find out about the joyful parts of themselves. Those parts are really there all the time, and people can appreciate themselves and affirm each other's existence and humanness. There are not many structures in our society for doing that, which is why we're involved in creating and leading cooperative play opportunities.

- Joel: Let's take off on this point of helping people to feel good and to cooperate. These seem to be two of your main goals. Can you give an example of a popular game today that goes against those goals?
- Pamela: We went to a party a few weeks ago that was specifically a charades party. Before we actually started playing charades, I talked with three or four of the people who seemed really friendly. We were having very nice interactions. Then, we started laying the ground rules for charades, and it went from that into a whole evening where there was much tension. There was one man, who, if I had not spent some time with him beforehand, would have been hard for me to see as a kind, wonderful person. He was very caught up in the game during the whole night.

   Husbands and wives, good friends, coworkers were all lashing out at each other. It was amazing—there was no attempt to see each other as human beings and there was just such antagonism. Then, at the end of the night, after the game was all over, everyone immediately got up to go home and didn't interact with each other at all. It was so clear that there was so much pain involved in what was supposed to be a fun Saturday night. The intention was for them to all get together and have a good time, but the game pitted them against each other in such negative ways.
- Matt: People in many traditional games situations exhibit behavior that is the antithesis of supportive. People are rewarded for pointing out other people's mistakes. A certain language of derision is the status quo in playing conventional games. People who are used to being really kind to each other lose sight of the fact that there are other human beings in the game and just humiliate other people and make them feel horrible.

   What we try to do is give people a different kind of vocabulary for playing with each other, so they can realize that their purpose in coming together is not to play a game. The purpose is to use games as tools to reach out to other people and to exhibit the best parts of themselves—the joyful, playful parts, and to make contact with the same parts in other people.
- Joel: So, people got so caught up in the charades game and its rules that they lost sight of themselves, others, and the original purpose of the activity, which was to have fun and interact with people. Given that type of situation—a game that seems to legitimize putting the rules before people, what would you suggest? Would you suggest not playing that game at all, or is there some way of modifying it so that it could be a more positive, constructive opportunity for people to make contact with one another?
- Pamela: I think that many times you can change the game in a way that will make it more fun. We used to give people a chance to concentrate on "What are you liking about this game?", "How can we make that the focus of the game?", and "How can we do even more of that?" For instance, if what you like is getting up and running around the room, how can we build more of that into the game?
- Joel: It seems that your objectives are to help people take control of the games they play, and, in a larger sense, to help them take control over their own lives by

cooperating with others. Can you describe another game in which people have a chance to work with one another?

- Matt: Big Ball Volleyball is played with a ball that is three feet in diameter, so that no matter what your skills are, it's almost impossible to do much by yourself. No one has the strength or agility to do it alone. So, by its very nature, it is cooperative. When that big ball is falling, you need many hands on it to keep it up in the air.

  That particular game is usually the last one in a sequence in which we use the three-foot ball. We start with people passing the ball around in a circle to each other, then passing it over their heads and down a line—where each person keeps running to the back of the line to keep the ball moving down the field. There's a lot of cooperative play with everyone handling the ball and giving it to other people before we start hitting it in the air. We first play with it in a way that everyone really can have control of it by giving it to other people.

  Actually, we don't play that game anymore, mainly because of a personal choice we made to stop using any equipment. The reason for that is that when a game centers around a piece of equipment, it's much easier for people to forget that they've come there to be with other people, and to make joyful contact with them. Instead, they get sucked into "the game" by shoving people out of the way, so they can get their hands on the ball. The big ball becomes the focus of everyone's attention, rather than each other. In lots of ways, that's antithetical to our goals.

  It's a tricky problem: playing with equipment like the ball or the three-way-tug-of-war rope is great fun, but it's difficult to facilitate the interactions that we want to see happening between people. When people come up to us afterwards and say, "Hey that was wonderful, where can we get a ball like that?", we feel happy that they had such a good time, and yet disappointed that their attention is on the equipment rather than on the other people. So, that's why we don't use much equipment anymore.

- Joel: How do you spread the word on this new perspective about games and playing?
- Matt: Playfair is the name of the games event that we present when we tour colleges. It's about a two-hour sequence of facilitated games—cooperative ones, not competitive ones. The idea is that by playing together, people can get to know each other better. A feeling of community can arise out of a play-situation. We're mostly brought in by colleges to work/play with a specific group of people—such as a freshman class for their orientation program or a student leadership retreat.
- Joel: You talk about being invited by colleges, where you do most of your work. Are Playfairs adaptable for developing a community in camps, schools, or in family groups?
- Matt: I think they have tremendously wide application. We've worked with a number of organizations, including senior citizens groups, schools, outdoor education programs, Campfire Girl counselors, and churches. For instance, one church was having their annual fellowship dinner and told us that it had always been a failure. The members always sat by themselves. The church leaders thought they would try a Playfair to mix the various people. By its very nature, Playfair gets people playing with other people. For the first time, members who were afraid to approach

strangers were put in a situation where they were with people they didn't know—and actually got to know them.

I think it is important to develop a safe climate in which people can interact physically with each other. By stressing the noncompetitive nature of the games that we play, we reach a lot of people who have stopped playing games in their lives, because they do not feel good enough to compete.

When I was in high school learning the trampoline, I didn't participate right away. By the time I got up enough nerve to try it, I was behind everybody else. They could do fancy flips while I was ashamed to admit that I had to learn the basics. The gap just got wider and wider, until it was impossible for me because of peer pressure to ever get up on the trampoline. I think that is an important difference with Playfair. People can re-enter, safely and supported, into physical activity with us, without having to worry about skill differences.

Also, we have been able to defuse some existing games that are predicated on skill differences and give people a chance to play them again. Tag is a good example of that. There are lots of problems with the old game of tag. One is that if you run fast, you don't get caught; and if you run slowly, then you're "it" for a long time. We've been able to do a lot of different things to tag to make it a number of different games, in which the tension about performance and skill is not there.

For example, to deal with the differences in speed and agility, we play a lot of Slow-Motion Tag. In slow motion, you'll get caught sooner or later. Also, we play Blob Tag, in which instead of trying to get rid of "it," it's okay to be "it." In fact, every time you tag someone, that person joins up with you and becomes part of "it," and the game ends when everyone is "it."

Often, we play Switch-Team Tag, which involves two opposing teams. When you get caught, instead of being penalized or eliminated, you move over to the other team. One team will eventually grow so big that is encompasses the other team, and the game ends when there is only one team—the winning team. In that kind of situation, where the only "penalty" is that you move from one team to the other, people feel the safety to experiment with new types of behaviors.

- Joel: You have a commitment to providing opportunities for people to experiment and make games a laboratory for learning. It is also important for you not to eliminate people, so that in a game of tag, everybody stays in the game.

- Pamela: There are lots of opportunities during the Playfairs for people to do things that they ordinarily wouldn't try. For instance, running in slow motion can be fabulous fun, but the average person doesn't usually get a chance to try it. Not only do we make that part of the game, but everybody does it. Nobody is watching you, because everyone is doing it themselves. We work hardest at helping everyone feel included and helping everyone learn how to include other people.

- Joel: Four principles were coming across very strongly to me in what you were just saying. One is the notion of equity—when you were talking about the guideline of everybody going in slow motion, there's a real feeling of equity. Second, it seems that people would be conscious of self, but not self-conscious. They are aware of themselves and their own experience of trying out new things, but the situation is safe enough that they don't feel self-conscious or that they're in a fishbowl. Third, you emphasize inclusion, rather than exclusion. The fourth, I would assume, is that you're trying to get people actively involved in their own recreation, so that instead of watching the slow motion instant replay on a football game on TV, they experience slow motion themselves. What are some of the other principles you use in designing Playfair experiences?

- Matt: We start with games in which our leadership is strongest. We direct the participants in playful experiences, give them strong guidelines as to what they should do, and move them quickly from one thing to another. One of our principles is that we almost always play first and talk later. People's attention for hearing theoretical presentations and the philosophical guidelines behind our work is much stronger after they've played a little, loosened up a bit, and laughed. By playing first, and then talking about our philosophy and what we expect to do, we give people a common base of the Playfair concept.

  Then, we let people think about their own particular histories of playing. We structure sharing, in which people talk one-to-one about how they grew up playing, about what kinds of games they played, and about pleasant memories they have of games. We move on from there to do some group games and then some partner games. We might teach 10 different games in a 45-minute period to be played with 10 different partners.

  The progression goes from games where we have control to ones where the participants have more control and leadership. This factor is an important principle about the games we design. They are games in which we set up broad outlines of what can be done, but then we no longer give the commands or take over the leadership—it's open for anyone to take over. Subsequently, people start coming out of the ranks, giving directions, and helping other people. There is an excitement not only about playing, but also about creating and leading at the same time. I think we've been very successful in developing those kinds of structures for games.

- Pamela: I want to address your initial question about Playfair principles. I want people to be up and moving right away. The first things they do should be physical, but not threatening.

  Matt was talking about how we gradually let the participants take over the leadership. There's a game called Touch Blue that reflects this progression. When I first learned the game, it went like this: when the leader says, "touch blue," everybody touches blue on another person; when the leader says "touch red," everybody touches red on another person; the leader continues to give directions, and everybody follows. That was the whole game. My first thought was that this was not very active. Why not let people move around in between, so there would be a locomotion element? I would then say, "touch blue" followed by a command of how to move around (e.g., skip, hop, jump). The next step in my thinking was, "Why should I be the only one to dream up all the things to touch and the ways to move? I want to play, too." So, I set up the structure to allow any of the players to say what the commands would be.

- Joel: This factor seems to reinforce the principle of equity—the leaders participate as well—the leaders are players, even though at the beginning of the Playfair, you would offer specific structures so that people wouldn't flounder. I'm wondering if you could give me some examples of some games you might play at the beginning—the ones that would have more specific instructions or directions—and then give an example of a game that might occur toward the middle—and then one that might be more open-ended and occur near the end.

- Pamela: There's a game called Incorporations, in which the leader shouts out commands of kinds of groups for people to get into. The game is about forming and reforming groups. We might say, "get into a group of three," or "get into a group of three plus one," or "get into a group of people who were all born in the same month." People are told exactly what to do by the leader. We participate in the game, and also are the ones calling out the categories of groups. This game allows people to be with many different people, totally based on random categories that are safe and don't threaten anybody.

Rawpixel/iStock/Thinkstock

- Joel: It sounds like one of those fast-paced games where people are up and moving. There's a chance for them to get to know other people with whom they might not have associated before. When you get together with other people who have the same astrological sign or are wearing the same color, that's usually a random grouping.

- Matt: There's another game that follows this same principle of grouping people in categories. In this game, the responsibility moves from the leaders to the players. The game is called Big Wind Blows. We play it with a parachute. In this activity, the group asks the question, "What does the big wind blow?", as they lift the parachute over their heads. One person calls out a category—for instance, "everybody born in May," then everyone born in May runs underneath the parachute and changes places with someone else before the parachute comes down.

Besides the fun involved in running underneath a billowing parachute, the game creates that same feeling of belonging with people. Examples of other ways to cluster people could include such categories as: "everyone who is wearing sneakers," "everyone who wears glasses," or "everyone who had scrambled eggs for breakfast." It is fun for people to see other individuals who belong in that coincidental category with them. It is up to the members of the group to think of the commands to get everyone moving.

- Joel: What happens if somebody calls out a random grouping that you might think is not positive? Is there anything you can do to guard against that?

- Pamela: One of the most important principles is to tell people ahead of time that they may not call something like, "everyone who is too fat." We tell them, "take charge of yourself, and don't do that. Remember that you want people to feel good about running under the parachute."

- Joel: Can you give us other examples of games that might be used near the beginning as loosener-uppers or get-to-know type games?

- Matt: Three Positions is a good game at the beginning. In this activity, we divide the participants into three different teams. If we were working with a group of 60, we would divide them into three teams of 20. We would then solicit from the group three different positions that any person could hold for a few seconds. The positions are physically simple enough, so that people can do them (for instance, standing on one leg, scratching your kneecap, rubbing your stomach). With that repertoire of three different positions, each team huddles and picks one. Then, on a given count, they come out and show the position. The object of the game is for all three teams—without ever talking to each other—to do the same position at the same time.

One of the good things about starting with a game like that is that it gives people a chance to talk with each other and make decisions. It also gives people a sense of solidarity by doing something all together and working toward a common goal. In addition, there's a great sense of joy, if after a few rounds, people figure out a strategy, and all three teams do the same thing.

We also let people other than ourselves do the countdown. We have a lot of funny ways of counting, rather than just 1-2-3 … we'll do it on the count of "carrot"—and count off "soybean, potato, carrot." Subsequently, other people pick up on that funny way of counting, and it gives people a creative way to announce to the group when it is time to show their position.

- Joel: A couple of principles seem to be important in this game: a chance for laughter (from creative counting) and a cooperative goal structure (from having all three teams try to demonstrate the *same* physical position). This situation contrasts with a competitive philosophy in which one position is more powerful than another—as in the popular rock-scissors-paper game.

- Pamela: The counting method gives people the idea that we're playing around with game structures, that they are not sacred. It is another way of saying that "1-2-3" is not the only way to count—that sometimes you can count to "string beans." That's an important point to get across from the beginning.

- Joel: How about another example of a game that you might use near the beginning as an energizer?

- Matt: One principle that we're concerned with is letting people know each other's names. Sometimes—and people love to do this—we have people go around and pretend they are the host or hostess at a party. Everyone here has been invited to the party, but no one knows each other's names. We give participants two minutes to introduce every person there to every other person. People are collaring individuals, finding out their names, bringing them over to someone else, introducing them. There's a lot of handshaking and laughing, and people meeting their best friends as if they never knew them before. Playing Introductions is a real good way to have physical contact and an excuse to ask, "What's your name?"

- Joel: When you say giving people an excuse, what you're really doing is giving people permission to do some things that, in many cases, they'd like to do, but are afraid to do. This seems to be an important Playfair principle. Can you give an example of another game that "gives people permission?"

- Pamela: Elbow Fruit Hop asks people to do things that are outrageous and silly. Usually, adults don't want to be silly, or they think they don't. It's a game in which one person gives a series of commands, e.g., a part of your body to touch, a category of objects that you would say over and over again, a way to move around, etc. For example, everybody might hold onto their stomachs, saying the name of a city, while jumping, until somebody changes the three commands.

- Joel: How does a participant change the commands?

- Pamela: We have a whistle that people come over and blow (or you could use a cowbell). Depending on the size of the group, we sometimes use the whistle with a microphone. It is important that they know where to go for the whistle. It stays in one place within the playing area, so they don't have to run across the field to change the commands. Once people realize that if they're tired of hopping around, it is their responsibility to change the commands into something that they feel like doing.

    It's loads of fun to see people walking or crawling around, holding their noses, and saying "asparagus" over and over. The basic principle is to establish a norm in which everybody gets to do it, so no one feels stupid. It's a way for people to be boisterous and not feel self-conscious about it.

- Joel: What you're doing is legitimizing having fun, being silly, and letting the kid in everyone come out and play. I take it the name of the game comes from the three elements that the people would do: the elbow is an example of a part of the body, fruit could be one of the categories, and hop is one example of a physical movement.

- Pamela: Elbow Fruit Hop is also an example of a game in which we set up a structure for people to end it. We tell people at the beginning, "If you want to end the game, then the commands you call out are elbow, fruit, hop." In other words, stating the name of the game is the way to end it. That happens in a number of our games. The underlying principle behind this factor is that people are more likely to remember the name "elbow fruit hop," if they use it in the game.

I'd like to say something about "letting the kid come out and play." Being silly and laughing a lot may have the connotation of being "childish," but what we're saying is that it's okay to be like that, to do things like that when you're over 30. Our hope is that people will not come away from a Playfair thinking, "Well, I acted like a kid today; now, I have to go back acting like an adult." We hope they will say, "I was an adult all day today, and I laughed and had a fabulous time with myself and others."

The intention of Playfair is not for you to act like a child, but rather to be yourself and to experience a sense of your own playfulness.

- Joel: I like the notion of focusing on the playfulness in us—getting away from the Peter Pan notion that when you reach a certain age, you lose your playfulness. You're not asking people to return to being Peter Pan, but rather tapping the play-fullness in them at whatever age they are. How about one more example of a game that brings out playfulness in people?

- Matt: We've adapted a game called Animals, from the New Games Foundation. In this activity, we solicit three different animals and the sounds they make from the group. We ask people to pick one of those, and then, with their eyes closed, to make the sound of the animal they picked. They then try to get together with everyone else who has picked the same animal. Of course, we have a few people standing outside to stop people from walking away from the crowd and to help people get together. There's always great laughter accompanying that game.

- Joel: One principle you mentioned is important—having people engage in "spotting," particularly if the games involve some sort of physical risk. To ensure people's physical safety in Animals, some people should have their eyes open.

- Matt: It is safer for the people walking around with their eyes closed, if they know that there will be some people around with their eyes open to make sure that they don't walk into walls or poles. People don't have to worry that they're walking in the wrong direction and that people will laugh at them. A lot of these risks are eliminated.

- Joel: The games you have described so far are for groups of people. I'm wondering if you can give some illustrations of cooperative games that two people could play together as partners and how they are paired.

- Matt: It's fun and very important to invent nonthreatening ways to help people find partners. It's difficult to just say, "Okay, pick a partner," or "Pick the person you'd most like to play with," because that brings up all sorts of feelings of embarrassment and panic for some people. We've thought of lots of good random ways to get people with partners, so that there's little tension. For example, "Put from zero to five fingers in the air, walk around, and see what everyone else is holding up. Pick a partner so that your fingers, when added, result in an even number." Or, "Find a partner who's wearing the same number of rings as you are." The list is virtually endless.

It's also fun to adapt games that are usually played in groups to two-person games. Leapfrog, for example, can be played by two people, with one leaping over the other. We do many physical type games with partners. One, for example, is called Off-Balance. The object of the game is for both people to support each other, and yet to be continually off-balance. There's a lot of movement, leaning on each other, pulling away from each other—but always as a coordinated type of movement exercise.

- Joel: Unlike competitive arm wrestling, the object is to be off-balance and yet make a cooperative effort, so that one person isn't the "winner" and the other the "loser."
- Matt: Both participants are off-balance the entire time, and yet no one falls at all. Both people support each other the whole time.

There's another game called Human Spring. In this activity, two partners stand about three to four feet apart with their palms out in front of their chests. They lean into each other, touch hands, and then spring back. The idea is for them to keep their balance. It's a coordinated springing back and forth, with the option of varying the distance between them.

There's also a partner game based on the Italian counting game, Morra. In this game, each of the partners makes a fist. On a given count, each participant can put out from zero to five fingers. The object of the game is to guess the total number of fingers that will be displayed. The total could range from zero to 10, depending on what you and your partner put out. That originally is a competitive game, in which the first one to guess right wins. We usually play it so that when you and your partner have a total of three correct guesses between you, then you've both "won."

It's fun to add variations. You can play with two hands and get up to 20 possible numbers, or play with four people, each using one hand. The more people who play, the harder it is to make a correct guess.

- Joel: How are the partner games usually played in Playfair situations? How do you structure them?
- Pamela: Sometimes, we divide people randomly into pairs, and then ask them to label themselves (e.g., "scrambled eggs" and "fried eggs"). Then, we arrange the people into two concentric circles, with pairs facing one another (e.g., the fried eggs on the outer circle facing in, and the scrambled eggs on the inner circle facing out). We teach one partner game, and after playing it, we'll ask the fried eggs to move three people to their right. So, each person quickly goes on to another partner.

Then, we teach another game. People can learn eight different partner games quickly and play them with eight different partners. We also give people some free choice. Randomly matched up with a partner, they get to pick which of those games they want to play. People have a repertoire of games to play when they get together with that new person.

- Joel: This sequence seems to use the principle you mentioned earlier. You provide some structure first and then give people a choice about which game(s) they would like to play. The group games and the partner games would be placed earlier in a Playfair. What do you do near the end to bring some closure to the experience?
- Matt: We always give people a chance to talk with each other, sometimes to share highlights of what's happening to them there, sometimes to talk about what's good

in their lives outside the Playfair. We always like to end by giving people a chance to verbalize their appreciations for how the day has gone. One game for doing that is called Wonderful Circle. In this activity, people put their arms around each other's waists, and move in a circle, taking small steps. Whenever someone has something wonderful they want to talk about (e.g., something they appreciate about the leadership, something they discovered about their own playfulness), they can stop the circle and speak. The circle moves around to the left until someone says, "stop." That person would say one positive thing and then say, "go." The circle would then move around to the right until someone else says, "stop."

- Pamela: When we work with smaller groups, we often use a different format for a closing. We ask people to sit in a circle and share, one-by-one, some specifics about what they appreciated during the Playfair. We usually give some pretty clear guidelines about what they could focus on—e.g., their own participation in interactions with other people, positive characteristics of the group, etc. We think it is important for people to say out loud what they felt good about.

- Joel: In closing this interview, I would like to let you know that I really appreciate the creative perspective you bring to playing. I believe that if we can help young people and adults to play together positively, cooperatively, and joyously, we will have a significant impact on how they play "the game of life."

PLAY IT AGAIN, MATT!

Matt Weinstein is the solar system's foremost authority on the use of fun and humor in team building. Known as "America's Pied Piper of Play" and called "The Master of Playfulness" by *PEOPLE* magazine, Matt is the founder and emperor of Playfair, an international consulting firm that does presentations for more than 100,000 people each year. Matt's playful vision has been the subject of dozens of national newspaper articles, magazine features, and television appearances, including *The Wall Street Journal, The New York Times, Today,* and *CBS This Morning.*

Matt was elected by the National Speakers Association to the CPAE Speaker Hall of Fame and was honored by *Successful Meetings Magazine* as one of the "21 Top Speakers for the 21st Century." His television special, *FUN WORKS!: The Power of Humor in the Workplace,* was broadcast nationally on PBS. Matt is the author/co-author of five books— *Managing to Have Fun; Gently Down the Stream: Four Unforgettable Keys to Success in Life and Work; Dogs Don't Bite When a Growl Will Do: What Your Dog Can Teach You About Living a Happy Life; Work Like Your Dog: How to Work Less, Play More, and Earn More; and PLAYFAIR: Everybody's Guide to Noncompetitive Play,* co-authored with Joel Goodman.

Joel delights in and is amazed at his dear friend Matt's creative energy, his sweet heart, and his ability over the decades to mobilize and bring together an amazing team that is the Playfair staff. Matt is an awe-inspiring, motivational, and humorous professional speaker who has dazzled many corporate, college, and TED audiences.

He has appeared as a featured keynote speaker and drew rave reviews a number of times at the international conference on "The Positive Power of Humor and Creativity," sponsored by Joel's organization, The HUMOR Project.

Years after our initial aforementioned interview, we were happy to have Matt give us a quick update on Playfair and to point out some valuable current resources related to cooperative play.

- Joel: So, in a nutshell, give us a quick take on what has Playfair been up to lately.
- Matt: Our work with colleges and universities has been constantly expanding, so we now work with more than 400 colleges and universities each year, doing playful "team building"—networking events for new-student orientation at the beginning of the school year. There are also many other organizations who ask Playfair for these same type of large-scale, playful community-building events—whenever organizations want a fun, upbeat, safe way for their participants to quickly meet and interact. Those organizations include staff trainings for camps and school districts, association conferences, and corporate meetings. In addition, we work with inmates in prisons, as well as with campers at summer camps at the beginning of the season. We also put our philosophy to work in the corporate world, with interactive, upbeat keynote talks about "How to Have More Fun at Work."

"Work consists of whatever a body is obliged to do. Play consists of whatever a body is not obliged to do."

—Mark Twain

GIVING CREDIT WHERE CREDIT IS DUE

You can find many videos and articles about Playfair's unique approach to team building and noncompetitive play at www.Playfair.com, for example:

- Playfair's founder Matt Weinstein demonstrates the use of play in recovering from personal loss in his TED talk: https://www.ted.com/talks/matt_weinstein_what_bernie_madoff_couldn_t_steal_from_me
- Playfair's unique and impactful work with inmates in prison are featured in this TEDx talk: https://www.youtube.com/watch?v=TXwH3SIF9rc
- For more information about Playfair and for descriptions of 60 exciting cooperative games (as well as the magical keys to inventing your own), see Matt Weinstein and Joel Goodman's classic book, *Playfair: Everybody's Guide to Noncompetitive Play*, published by Impact Publishers, 1980.
- For many more cooperative activities, be sure to see our companion book, *201 Nature and Human Nature Activities*, which is described at the beginning of the Resources chapter in this book.

CHAPTER 8
CREATIVE LEADERSHIP: A HUMANISTIC APPROACH TO COACHING

"When they start the game, they don't yell, 'Work ball!'
They say, 'Play ball!'"

—Baseball Hall-of-Famer Willie Stargell

You already "met" Jeff McKay in Chapter 5. He returns in this chapter for an encore appearance with insights on creative leadership and humanistic coaching. In addition to serving as associate director at NFL Hall of Famer Benny Friedman's national quarterback camps and head football coach at Millbrook School, Jeff is a diamond and has spent a lot of time around the diamond. He has held baseball coaching positions at many levels, including Little League, California Lutheran University, University of California, University of Massachusetts, Middlebury College, and Amherst College. Jeff has served as lead trainer for the Positive Coaching Alliance and has been a mentor coach to the San Francisco Giants and the St. Louis Cardinals Major League baseball teams. In addition, he has taken himself and baseball abroad as the Major League Baseball International Envoy Coach in Great Britain, France, Moldova, and Sweden. Jeff is founder and director of Be Your Own Coach.

One of the most traditional forms of outdoor activity in our country has been sports. To realize how pervasive an influence sports are in our culture, we need only take a look at baseball as "our national pastime," the Super Bowl societal saturation, the NHL and NBA playoffs, college basketball's "March Madness," and even the 2016 World Series that captured the nation's attention as the Chicago Cubs finally won the title after 108 years.

What follows is an interview that Joel Goodman conducted with Jeff decades ago that focused on ways that we can humanize sports. As you will see, it is both timeless and timely. A significant part of Jeff's success comes from his effectiveness in applying humanistic education guidelines and principles to his coaching. In the conversation, he suggests a number of innovative approaches to mixing the following ingredients in athletics: challenge, cooperation, individual excellence, joy, and learning. As a bonus, we will go into extra innings as Jeff shares his recent thoughts and experience on coaching that could apply to any sport.

- Joel: Let's start by taking a look at some of the roles you've had in coaching.
- Jeff: When I was in college, I worked for a man named Bennie Friedman, who was a pro quarterback back in the old days. I worked as his assistant at a national football camp for quarterbacks and pass receivers for about six years. One of the things I learned from Bennie is the concept that a player needs to be his own coach. To me, that's a nugget that's been worth developing.

  My first formal kind of coaching experience in an institution was at a small secondary school in New York, where I coached football and baseball. I was doing things in ways that my experience had taught me, and it wasn't particularly enjoyable. Then I moved to California and coached football and baseball again. I remember that the football coach at our school, Bob Schaup, was highly successful. One of the good things I learned from Bob was the idea of having fun. The day before the biggest game of the year, the players were very tense over what would happen. Bob had them playing volleyball over the football goal posts. Part of me said, "That's crazy." But there was another part saying, "Hey, this guy's onto something."

I then took a year off from my involvement in athletics. As I look back on it, the time and space away from athletes allowed me to cast off many attitudes and approaches that were unduly old for me. I came back to athletics a year later with more openness and freshness. I got involved at the University of California, coaching the freshman-sophomore team. I started experimenting. I wanted to try some new things. So, I started fooling around with coaching through experimentation—giving players a voice in how we practiced. It was a very exciting time for me.

At this point, two things influenced me. One was an involvement with Esalen Institute's Sports Center—where I explored the martial arts, talked about improving athletes as a human endeavor, and met Tim Gallwey, who has developed the "inner game of tennis." The second influence was meeting George Davis, a beautiful man, who, at the time, was coaching football in northern California. He used football as a vehicle for creating almost a pure Athenian democracy.

I've also spent two years coaching the freshman-sophomore team and one year working with the varsity at the University of Massachusetts. I've had a chance to further develop some of the directions I was taking that started in California.

- Joel: If you had to summarize the kernel of your philosophy, based on these different experiences, what would it be?

- Jeff: I see sports and athletics as a holistic experience that involves mind, emotion, and body. The possibilities for personal growth and learning in a traditional sense are almost boundless. I would like to facilitate in my athletes a sense of personal growth and the ability to fully participate in a joyful activity.

- Joel: I'd like to probe a little deeper into the philosophy underlying your interest in humanizing sports. What are your guiding principles in coaching?

- Jeff: I start with what I call individual excellence. My feeling is that my first job as a player is to do my own best; and my job as a coach would be to help someone to move toward individual excellence. That means that individual excellence even comes before team, which is a little different from the way some coaches might think. I like to start out with the idea of individuals challenging themselves to achieve excellence, which has nothing to do with statistics. I also put a lot of emphasis on working together by stressing cooperation, as opposed to competition. Even people trying out for the same position can cooperate and help each other to improve.

- Joel: You're talking about dealing with cooperation and competition, not only interteam but also intrateam.

- Jeff: I think competition is a loaded issue. There's the Vince Lombardi school of thought, which says competition is everything and winning is everything. I don't buy that. There's another view, which says competition is evil and winning is nothing. I don't buy that either. I feel there's a comfortable, healthy middle ground. For you and me to compete—where you do your best and I do my best—isn't necessarily evil at all. With my teams, I try to emphasize us first, and to not concern ourselves particularly with the other team. Our job is to do our best, whether we're playing a poor team or a great team, our job is still to do our best. Our motivation is not based on whom we're playing. It's based on who we are. That has worked very well for me. To get a team up to play a really good team and to float through and play poorly against a bad team doesn't do anything for me.

I had an experience with the University of Massachusetts varsity in which we swept a doubleheader. The team we played wasn't very good. I talked to some of the players who felt that sweeping that particular doubleheader really was not a satisfying experience. I am saying that winning is not everything—it's the getting there that is really worthwhile.

- Joel: Your emphasis is in moving from either hollow victories, in which the focus is on beating the other team, to taking a look at winning victories within yourself, where you're competing with a standard of excellence within yourself or within the team.

- Jeff: There are three levels of moving from your individual excellence at second base to the cooperation of you and someone else at shortstop to competing with the other team at another level of cooperation. Our team's job is to do our best, and your team's job is to do your best—that's a cooperative contract between us. That's a beautiful concept for me.

The problem is that, at times, this contract is taken too far, and becomes: "Whoever wins takes all the marbles, and the loser gets nothing." I've really thought a lot about winning, because I think it's a crucial concept to address. One way most people judge success is to ask, "Did you win or lose?" I don't think that's the only way. It's possible to play very well and not win. Think about the runner who finishes in 10th place but beats his/her best time. That's a win! If you do your individual best, and I do mine, then winning becomes irrelevant.

- Joel: So, you're moving from looking at winning in a reverent fashion to looking at winning in an irrelevant fashion.

- Jeff: Another principle it has taken me a long time to learn is the idea that competitive sport can be fun. I think I had fun as a competitor. When I first became a coach, however, I thought that fun had nothing to do with it. I thought that it was a choice between winning or having fun. I don't believe that anymore. I also thought that the fun came from the winning; and if you lost, then all you had done wasn't fun.

As a coach, I try to incorporate some fun into what we do. For example, we have relay races at the end of practice and a home-run hitting contest once a week. I've tried to structure fun into our practices so that after we work very hard, the players and I have a release.

Many athletes have an inclination to fool around. For me, it's important to separate the fooling around from the hard work. One way I can do that is to legitimize "fun" on certain occasions.

- Joel: What you're moving toward is the concept of unconditional fun … fun that is not based on whether you win or lose, but on how you play the game. Do you have any other principles?

- Jeff: One of the things I believe very strongly about athletics is that it should be an educational experience. That means that the player has a large say in what happens. When I get players coming from high school, in many cases, what they want to do is to perform for the coach. I try to help them see that they should perform for themselves first, and their teammates and me second.

- Joel: Instead of trying to psyche out the coach, the players are setting their own personal goals of excellence and trying to meet those and, at the same time, working cooperatively with their teammates. What you're talking about is viewing the player as umpire, in the sense of making internal decisions, evaluations, and judgments about certain issues.

- Jeff: I am concerned about coaching individual people, as well as coaching the team, and allowing for individual people to have idiosyncrasies and to do things differently. I don't feel it's at all necessary for everybody on the team to look the same or do this the same or hit with the same kind of stance. It strikes me as counterproductive. Everybody's different physically. Everybody's different in their head. To the extent that we can take that factor into consideration in athletics, people will do better. More importantly, people will have a better time.

- Joel: The times when I've played on coach-oriented or coach-disciplined teams, as long as the coach was there hanging over your head, you got down to it. The norm that developed in that situation, however, is that when the coach turned his back, that's when players started messing around. What you're talking about is— regardless of whether the coach has his eyes on you or not, you're your own boss, and you direct yourself.

- Jeff: Right. There are some implications of that, too, for the coach. For example, one thing that I work at—and I'm not sure how close to it I get—is to get away from being a coach all the time. There's a tendency for me, since I know how to grip a curve ball, to teach somebody how to grip a curve ball. I think in the long run, it's going to be much more successful if I can help that person experiment and have him learn how to throw a curve ball, rather than to have me teach him how to throw a curve ball. My guess is that, when it's the bottom of the ninth, and the heat's on, he's going to remember it much better if he learned how to do it himself, rather than having me teach him.

That's one of the beauties of this when we come back to the question of success. Yes, it does work; and I think, in the long run, it pays off. The player can learn a lot without me getting in the way. That's not to say that I don't need all the skills and all the resources in order to be able to help him, but that I use those when appropriate, rather than always teaching and coaching in a dogmatic sense.

There's another part to it, too, which is to try to help players to become their own coaches; that takes a while. My experience as an athlete and the experience of lots of athletes I'm working with currently is that they have their own "coach," and their coach is their head getting in the way of their body. Somebody is having trouble hitting. Subsequently, he comes to me and says, "Is my weight too far forward? Do I need to cock my wrists a little more? Am I moving my head? Am I moving away from the plate?" Can you imagine trying to remember all of those factors and hit the ball at the same time?

- Joel: *Zen and the Art of Archery*—revisited.

- Jeff: I'm not denying the coach's need for being knowledgeable in all those areas. It's just that, in many cases, we need to clear out the space inside the head to allow the athlete's body to perform naturally and then help with some refinements and some minor adjustments. The thought of being able to teach somebody how to hit is more than I can bite off, as well as more than most people can process.

- Joel: You talked about coaching individuals. Do you also have a principle that relates to coaching a team? How do you help a group of individuals to get together into a team? Is that important to you?

- Jeff: Yes, that's very important. One of the beauties of sport, to me, is the camaraderie—building a community. What I'm interested in doing is creating a team that is the players' team and not just my team. This premise is not that way-out a concept. What I'm concerned with is moving gradually from a coach-dominated team to a player-run team. My experience is that such a scenario has to be gradual, because most players' experience has been "Tell us what to do, coach."

  One of the first things we do is to elect player representatives, which is almost the same as electing captains. The difference for me is that, rather than electing captains at the end of this year for next year, we'll start next year with who we have and elect from that group. It seems more present tense. Those player representatives get involved in a variety of decisions, such as, "What do we need to work on in practice? Do we take a day off this week? When do we take a day off this week? Do practices need to be longer or shorter?"

  These kinds of decisions are normally made by the coach. In many cases, their decision is the same as mine; and in many cases, they have good ideas that I hadn't thought of. So, it's not a question of their taking over my responsibilities. It's a question of all of us being responsible.

  I also have the players involved in decision-making about rules and regulations. I can remember the first time we did this at the University of Massachusetts many years ago. One of the player representatives was a tremendous leader, so I turned the show over to him to develop the rules and regulations, the dress code, etc. He got up in front of the group, and he started laying on the team: "I think we ought to do this and that!" I was sitting in the wing saying, "Oh, my God." During a break, I pulled the rep aside and said, "Time out. The point of this is to not have me run your lives. Furthermore, the point isn't for you to run their lives either." Athletes are not irresponsible. They just need an opportunity to take responsibility.

- Joel: This situation is another example of you trying to move from an authoritarian setup, in which the coach rules to the democratic vision that you mentioned earlier where there's participation and sharing of the responsibility.

- Jeff: Right. Another principle that's been particularly important is for me to learn from the players. I remember one day at California, I was walking out to practice and quite a few players were on the field early. One of the catchers was hitting infield practice to them. My first urge, as a coach, was, "Oh, you've got to get up there and take over for him, because the coach hits infield." Then I stopped myself and said, "There's nothing wrong with him hitting infield. In fact, they're having a great time!" The enthusiasm and the motivation that was going on in that situation was terrific. One thing I've learned from that is that player-run sessions—or, in a more generalized sense, player-initiated practice—is a tremendous idea. I've found that, to push the metaphor, they can take the ball and run with it.

- Joel: A common stereotype in our culture is that of "dumb jock." It occurs to me that one of the reasons that perception has developed is that in most sporting situations, the athletes are not allowed to think for themselves. They're always spoon-fed the directions from the coach—e.g., to steal or not to steal. What you're doing is having the athletes tap the information in their own computers and come up with the decisions for themselves.

- Jeff: The final step for me in the whole movement toward self-discipline is a concept that I learned from George Davis, whom I mentioned before. He has been using sport as a vehicle for creating a democratic enterprise for over 25 years. The underlying idea is, very simply, that it is our team, and the players need to be able to participate in that. So, what we do first is to have people decide where they want to play. I make sure that everyone knows that he has a shot at the place where he wants to play. So, if you want to play shortstop, fine, you try out for shortstop.

  The next step is that everyone chooses the starting lineup. That's a big jump and a beautiful jump, because what that says then is, "You are responsible for yourself and your teammates." Everybody on the team votes. The beauty of it is that it's a real strong message of, "Hey, my talk about it being your team is not just talk. Here you are."

  At first, the players find that a little bit difficult to deal with. Once they get used to it, however, it really becomes a growth experience in democracy for them. This country is a democracy, and, as such, we ought to be doing what we can in education and in sport to really foster that idea.

- Joel: The message that you're sending is that, literally and figuratively, they're responsible for the positions they're in and that you really do place faith, beyond the rhetoric level, in their ability to make decisions about in which positions, either individually or as a team, they place themselves.

  Could you say more about the players' reactions? I can certainly imagine that, after years of being in an authoritarian, "coach-knows-best" system, there might be some chaos and havoc at the beginning. How do you move from that? And does it work? That's a basic question to which a lot of coaches would say, "Hey, you can talk all up and down about this democracy stuff and that sounds great, but does it work? Do I keep my job as coach if the players are making those decisions for themselves?"

- Jeff: One of the exciting things is that it has worked. The first time I started the vote, I was afraid. I thought the players were going to vote for their friends and not pick the "right people." So, the first place for me to start was to be reasonably comfortable with myself in trying this out.

  I've had coaches say to me, "It all sounds nice, but aren't you really neglecting your responsibility? It's your job to plan practices." It is my job. The only thing I'm doing is

---

involving the players in the planning of practices, too. It's ultimately my responsibility. I don't see myself getting out of the responsibility, but taking on some more.

The same factor is also true of the vote. People may say, "That's really your responsibility to figure out who plays where, as well as who starts and who plays when." I don't think that's true. The vote certainly can be used in an advisory kind of capacity. But, the point of it is that I think it takes much more guts on my part to say, "Hey, here's a large piece of the pie. You guys see what you can do with it," than for me to say, "Do this. Do that. You play here. You play there."

I don't feel that it is a cop-out at all. I get angry when people say that I'm copping out. I also think that 20 people know better than one person. It's very possible that I may have a bias against a player of which I'm not even aware. As a result, I write him out of the starting lineup. On the other hand, when 20 people vote, these kinds of individual prejudices get cancelled out. That's a lot of what democracy is about. For me, it has worked very well.

- Joel: You see democracy as a risk, build that into your program, and accept the responsibility for that risk. You also follow the old adage of "two heads are better than one" (and 20 heads are better than one). You draw on the resources, the thinking, and the perspectives of everybody involved and do not limit your vision.

- Jeff: Another concern that I have and that people have expressed to me is, "How about the players? Can they deal with this?" I've talked with people about doing this on the college level, but they say, "Sure, it works in college, but it wouldn't work in high school or in the pros." I don't think that's right. It's probably easier, the older people get, because they're supposedly more mature and able to take more responsibility. It should be noted that this approach worked for George Davis in a high school situation. It has worked for me with college freshmen and seniors.

I don't think it's a question of age. I think it's a question of the coach being comfortable with it, and helping athletes to be comfortable with it. I like to challenge the athletes with the following: "Look, people have said to me that this won't work. The reason it won't work is that you're not mature enough, and you're not responsible enough. I say hogwash! It's up to you. Here's the ball." And they take off running.

- Joel: What about the people who are on a survivor level, who say: "This sounds great, but what about my job?" In other words, what kind of winning-losing record does this kind of system or approach produce? What has it produced for you?

- Jeff: It has always been successful. When I was at the University of California, with the freshman-sophomore team, we were 20 and 13, playing Pacific 8 level competition, and that was without a pitcher who had an E.R.A. below three. At the University of Massachusetts, the first year, we were 10 and 3; and my next year we were 14 and 4. So, it works.

In baseball, you either win a game or you lose it. And then, there are some in the middle. You either win 10 to 2 and clobber somebody, or you get beaten 8 to 1. Those games are not the ones that matter. The ones that matter are the ones where it's 5 to 5 in the bottom of the ninth. Those are the fun games. Those are the competitive games. Those are the thrilling games; and those are the ones, if you want to be a champion, you need to win. I can remember my first year at California—out of those 20 wins, we won six in the ninth inning by either breaking a tie or coming from behind. My feeling is that a lot of where that came from was the players' attitude of "we're in charge. We can make our decisions. This is our ball club." So, when it comes to the bottom of the ninth, it's not them performing for me or performing out of fear. It's them having faith in themselves.

- Joel: Let me get more into some specific scenarios and issues that would focus on the implications and applications of what you're suggesting. Let's take a very typical thing that occurs during a baseball game and other sporting events, razzing and trash talking going on between teams. How do you, as a coach, handle razzing?

- Jeff: I'd like to start by going back to the idea that our job, first of all, is to be responsible for ourselves individually and to take care of ourselves. All we owe to the other team is the respect of their being there. If a player on our club gets into razzing, I try to work with that person and help him not to do that. Our job is with us and our own excellence and our own competition. Razzing detracts from the game. It takes some energy away from us, and dissipates it in negative ways. We've got a full-time job of doing our best by putting all our energy and effort into picking ourselves up.

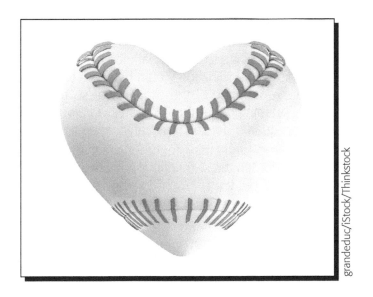

- Joel: What you're saying is that players ought to be playing "pick-up games," rather than "put-down games." Let me provide a second scenario. Let's say the focus, in this case, is the umpire. The umpire has just made, from our perspective, an awful call. The players are upset. You're upset. How do you deal with that? Part of this situation relates to the issue of "sportsmanship."

- Jeff: It's very unfortunate that we need umpires, first of all. If I were talking in a visionary sense, I would work to create a situation in which umpires are irrelevant. On the other hand, that's not the reality right now. What I try to do is to ignore the umpires, and to just concern ourselves with ourselves. While I have fallen victim to arguments with umpires, I think I'm getting closer to a situation where I'm just going ahead and playing the game and letting the chips fall. The chips include the umpire's decisions—right or wrong—bad or good. I have felt the need, at times, to protect my players; and that comes out of defensiveness and is something that I'd like to work through.

- Joel: Here's another issue: should everybody get to play? Or should only the best play? If you have a vote and the object is to field a winning team, does that mean that some players will never get off the bench?

- Jeff: That's a good, tough question—particularly for a competitive situation in which winning is something as opposed to everything or nothing. One of the ideas expressed by the old Boston Celtics, as much as anybody, is the idea of the whole bench being the "sixth man." I think that's a good concept. For me, that fits in with the concept of "pick 'em up."

    Starting doesn't mean anything more than starting and probably playing a majority of the game—not necessarily all the game. I think when push comes to shove, then it has to be my decision during the game with regard to, "Okay, do I give so-and-so a chance to play today?" Those are the kinds of decisions that I feel that I have to make—previously having had the players' input. On the other hand, during a game, I can't take time out to have a vote. If the game is one in which we're way ahead, it's no problem putting people in. The question is how soon? To put them in the ninth inning for a token appearance is better than nothing, but not much better than nothing. My inclination would be more to put them in during the sixth inning so they get a real bite of the experience—so they feel they can have some say in what's happening rather than to just show up at the end. Three plays at the end of the fourth quarter doesn't make any sense to me.

    Where it's tough for me—and I think for other coaches—is the decision of when you take the risk. If it's 5 to 3 in the sixth inning, so you say, "Well, we're only ahead by two runs," so you don't put them in? Or do you say, "Hey, we're ahead by two runs," so you put them in.

- Joel: What about the morale of those players who are third-string catchers?

- Jeff: One very helpful thing is that 90 percent of our practice consists of game situations, so that they are involved in real doing as much as is possible. Prior to the game, when we take infield and outfield practice, everybody on the team participates, rather than only nine guys going out and warming up with the other players being on the bench.

    In practice, we might play a short game in which, when the ball is hit, everyone on the defensive team has to touch the ball before a putout can be made. The point of that, in one sense, is everyone is important, everyone participates, and—on another level—it's fun.

    This factor makes me think of another thing that helps. When I first coached, I think I fell into the tendency to spend a lot of time with the number one pitcher—and progressively less time with the number two, number three, and number four pitchers. It's really easy to slip into that mindset. When I became aware of that, I made and continue to make a conscious effort to work with Joe Blow, who's the third-string catcher. For example, if he's having trouble with his hitting, I'll work with him after practice. That's a clear message—not so much in words, but in actions. This says to the third-string catcher, "Hey, he gives a hoot about me. I am a part of his team." I think that's really motivational.

- Joel: So, what you're really doing is providing equality of opportunity and equity in terms of your attention to players, regardless of whether they're the star of the club or the third-string batboy.

  Let me ask you this, Jeff. What gives you the greatest joy? What are some of the things that give you great joy in coaching? What's in it for you? What keeps you going and motivated?

- Jeff: One of the major things is having relationships with athletes and helping them to move toward self-motivation, self-reliance, and self-discipline. On a personal level, that has been a real good experience for me. On another level, I get real enjoyment from being successful in the way I go about it. It makes me feel good to think that I can break some new ground in approaches to coaching and the game—and to be successful at that.

- Joel: Let's imagine you could implement anything you wanted to in the world of sports or in the world of coaching. For instance, in baseball, how might you want to change the rules?

- Jeff: One would be to change the game, so that the goal would be not winning. If two teams did their best and were of equal ability, the ultimate goal could be to end up in a tie. This way of thinking smacks pretty hard against traditional views. I hope someday to become a commissioner of a Little League, in order to effect some positive changes.

- Joel: Okay, Mr. Commissioner. What advice would you give to some of the coaches in your league?

- Jeff: What would be necessary would be to find out where they are—each one individually. I would then try to help them move, so that they take less responsibility, and the children start to assume more responsibility. I would want them to realize that exerting pressure on a youngster, as I see it, rather than helping his performance, hinders his performance. The stereotype of the Knute Rockne speech to the little third-graders probably does more harm than good, not only to the child, but also as far as how well they do in the game. I shudder when I see young players, whose knees are shaking, who are worried about, "Boy, if I don't get a hit, the coach is going to knock my head off." Sports ought to be fun. I think that I would do a lot of crazy things—for example, games in which you hit with the opposite hand, running around the bases backward, etc.

- Joel: Let me ask you to look in a broader sense, beyond Little League, to the future of sports in general and more specifically to some of the hopes or visions you have for sports—where we might be heading with sports—what sports might look like in the year 2100.

- Jeff: Let me start off with where I'd like to see myself going, and then move to a more social vision. The score is tied 2 to 2, and it's the bottom of the ninth. One of our players hits a line-drive over the second-baseman's head. There are two out, and if it drops in for a base hit, we score a run and win; and if it's caught, the game's all over in a tie, or we have to go extra innings. The other team's second baseman makes an incredible play; and our whole team applauds him. That's where I'd like to get.

  I see the beautiful things going on in martial arts and in mind-body disciplines becoming more and more a part of American physical education. I see outdoor education growing by leaps and bounds. Lifetime sports and lifetime skills will also grow in popularity. I see some things coming out of the women's movement as being very healthy and exciting—less emphasis on winning, more concern for the person and how she feels, etc.

  I also look at the other side of the coin: sports are becoming ultra-commercialized; violence is increasing; football coaches are teaching linemen to hold. I've seen that happen. Money is running the game right now.

- Joel: In the *Tank McNamara* comic strip, a sportscaster comes up with examples of how kids are now playing baseball. It's not actually playing the game of baseball, but they start choosing up by saying something like, "Hey, I'll be the free agent. Hey, I'll be Bryce Harper's agent. Hey, I'll be Mike Trout's..." Do you have any closing personal reflections or thoughts that you might want to share?

- Jeff: I feel a need to make some kind of closing statement that refers to my personal experience and get off the cosmic pitch about what's right or wrong about athletics. Before I do that, I want to mention two books that have been helpful to me in moving in a direction that feels good to me. One is called *Zen and the Art of Archery*, which is about a German who goes to Japan to learn archery. He finds out from the masters that to learn archery he needs to learn Zen. There is a message in that for me—not only about a way of teaching—but also that archery isn't really what's important. What's important is what you can learn through archery about yourself and about others. I like to view baseball that way and to think that the other sports also have possibilities that help people move in that direction.

  The other reference I want to mention is called *Democracy and the Football Revolution: The Fifth Down*, which is written by Neil Amdor, a former sportswriter for *The New York Times*. The first half of the book deals with the abuses of recruiting and the overemphasis on winning. The second half of the book is entitled "Democracy," and it's about George Davis. It's an answer to those abuses and describes how George went about his experiment in Athenian democracy with young high school students, using football as a vehicle. That brings it full circle to me, because the abuses outrage me.

  At the present time, I feel moved beyond awareness of the abuses toward solutions—through democracy and through working with individuals. That's a good direction. That feels good. What I want to do is to continue to move along those lines and maintain my awareness of what I feel is oppressive, but put the focus on the beauty of sport. Sport can be an experience that helps people to learn about themselves and to move and to grow.

EXTRA INNINGS

- Joel: Jeff, it was exciting watching the Cubs win the World Series in extra innings, after 108 years. Well, it has not been 108 years since you and I first did the interview for this book, but it is still exciting, having a chance to go into extra innings with you!

    Since you last provided your inner views in the interview we did for the first edition of this book, what patterns or trends have you observed in sports?

- Jeff: The fact is we now have some big name coaches who "get" humanistic education—like Pete Carroll of the Seattle Seahawks, Steve Kerr of the Golden State Warriors, and Joe Madden of the Chicago Cubs—tells us that we have come a long way, baby. Both Carroll and Kerr are devotees of the "Inner Game," which introduced Western audiences to coaching, based on awareness and learning, rather than scripted content and teaching. The Inner Game was brought forward, back in 1975, by Tim Gallwey, around the same time that Zen master Phil Jackson was exploring his version of what Michael Murphy of the Esalen Institute called "sport as western yoga." There must have been something in the air.

- Joel: You have had experience as a coach from the Little Leagues with your son, Will, all the way up to the big leagues. What have you learned along the way?

- Jeff: My recent experience as a Little League coach tells me that we have a long way to go—or should I say—I have a long way to go. Trying to teach the Inner Game to 10-year-olds is more than a tall order. So, one of the main courses for me over the years is a sizable portion of humble pie.

- Joel: What other food for thought have you had about sports?

- Jeff: What I'm learning present-tense is that sports makes the connection between the mind and the body. Or, better said, between the body and the mind. In other words, the mind learns from the body, just as well as the body learns from the mind. That's the heart of the Inner Game, as I understand it.

- Joel: Are there tricks-of-the-trade you have found for nurturing the body-mind connection?

- Jeff: The key to the mind-body connection, as I practice it, includes: deep breathing with an exhale twice as long as the inhale; feeling one's connection with the Earth through the sensation of the feet on the ground; and centering—putting one's attention in the center of the body—your belly resource center, rather than lost in the mind's many thoughts. Try it, at least umpteen times a day. Repeat tomorrow and the next day.

- Joel: How do you help your players to keep their minds and bodies connected?

- Jeff: For me, as a coach, holding the perspective that sports are fun is a big-time challenge, especially when the players are under pressure. So, my guess is that we need to learn to practice sports as fun in practice, so that we might remember it in the cauldron of competition. That factor requires "embodied" learning. My experience, some of it through the School of Hard Knocks, is that learning happens two steps forward and one step back, if we're lucky. It's a process… and some of the time, it can be fun.

- Joel: Speaking of "under pressure," the seventh game of this year's World Series between Cleveland and Chicago was full of pressure and drama… and yet it was thrilling and fun to watch.
- Jeff: The Chicago Cubs' players-only meeting during the rain delay in Game 7 teaches us once again that the players are, in fact, in charge. I had a dramatic experience of this factor with the Middlebury College baseball team as a visiting coach. I had taught the players a pre-game centering routine. After being away from the club for more than a month, at the start of the first playoff game, I walked down the third base line to do the routine with them. One of the team leaders—the third-string catcher, mind you—stepped out of the circle to inform me that they had it on their own now, thank you, and needed me like a hole in the head. I swallowed my ego and returned to the dugout humbled and proud. Proud that they had learned what I profess—be your own coach!!!

   Presently, I am attempting to learn how to convey Be Your Own Coach to the Amherst College baseball team and the Swedish National Baseball Academy (no foolin'). And I am very aware that teaching Be Your Own Coach is not teaching, but finding creative ways to help the players learn how to be their own coaches.

- Joel: Jeff, you empower people in so many ways—both in baseball and sports and in the game of life.

"A ballplayer spends a good piece of his life gripping a baseball, and in the end, it turns out that it was the other way around all the time."

—Former Major League pitcher Jim Bouton

CHAPTER 9

HUMAN RELATIONS YOUTH ADVENTURE CAMP: A MODEL THAT REALLY WORKS

"If we are to reach real peace in this world, we shall have to begin with the children."

—Mohandas Gandhi

Creatas Images/Creatas/Thinkstock

The Human Relations Youth Adventure Camp (HRYAC) was founded in 1974 by Vera and Cliff Knapp and operated very successfully for many years as part of the National Humanistic Education Center in New York's Adirondack Mountains. The camp program was based on the belief that human interactions in a controlled setting can be influenced in a positive direction. The purpose was to create a small community in the wilderness.

For three weeks in August, approximately 24 boys and girls, ages 11 to 14, came together in a primitive setting. They lived in tents and shared the responsibilities of group living. At first, the only building was a one-room log cabin; later, it was a three-room building.

Among our basic assumptions were: everyone has the ability to relate to others with trust and caring; everyone has a zest for life, which is sometimes hidden, but is always there; everyone knows what is good for them, and they can learn to trust their inner wisdom; staff who have strong intrapersonal and interpersonal skills will help campers develop theirs; and campers learn to act maturely by being given choices and opportunities to control much of their own lives.

As this description of HRYAC unfolds, you will see how we integrated these assumptions into each day's activities. Are the assumptions about your program or curriculum apparent or hidden?

Certain elements essential to building a close community were considered in planning each day, including:
- *Trust and caring*—Trust in others, or a feeling of confidence in and security with people, must extend throughout the entire community for growth to occur. Campers must feel that the staff cares about them, and there must be someone around on whom each person can count. Campers and staff must be able to share concerns openly and have confidence in their abilities to work together toward common goals.
- *Respect for self and others*—Each person, staff and campers alike, must feel important to the successful functioning of the community. Each person's individuality is accepted and appreciated. All members of the community are treated as people whose needs and feelings are valued.
- *Cooperation and cohesiveness*—Cooperation must be reflected in the camp program. If activities are structured to foster group cohesiveness, the participants will evolve into a cooperative community. This goal does not merely happen—it must be carefully planned.
- *Opportunity for input*—Everyone in the community must feel that what they have to say will be heard and considered. They must feel a certain degree of power and control in their lives. No one will be a fully functioning person without the chance to influence the future.
- *Problem-solving and conflict resolution*—Problems and conflicts are natural and predictable occurrences in close living situations. They must be greeted with optimism and a belief that solutions will be found. A forum must be provided for problems and conflicts to be handled with rationality and nonviolence.

IN THE BEGINNING …

Our opening activities were designed to help everyone get acquainted. To trust people, we must first get to know them. Step one for us was to learn everyone's name. We accomplished this with 40 people in about 15 minutes, using a pillow-throwing game. We sat in a circle and tossed a pillow around. The one rule was that before the pillow was thrown to others, you must call them by name. If a person didn't know someone's name, it was fine to ask.

After learning names, we went around the circle, and each person answered a question such as, "If I could be magically changed into any kind of animal, what would it be, and why?" As people answered, they began to emerge as unique individuals.

An important concern at the beginning was, "Who will be my tentmates?" Instead of making assignments, we allowed the campers to group themselves. The process took a while, but it always worked out.

The next problem was, "Which tent will be ours?" The tents were already set up, and some sites were more desirable than others. Again, instead of telling the campers how to decide, we presented the situation as a group problem, and allowed the solutions of how to decide fairly to come from them. A more efficient method in terms of time and effort would have been to tell the campers what to do. Our thought was that by allowing the campers to make decisions important to their lives, we were demonstrating our confidence in their ability to think and decide, while building an atmosphere of trust and respect. Have you seriously considered when to tell campers what to do and when to let them decide for themselves?

We believed strongly that campers should have input into their scheduled activities. However, because we were concerned with developing the group into a cooperative, caring community, we designed some activities for the first few days that included everyone. One of these activities was a stream walk. We walked down the center of a rocky stream for about two miles. The water was often up to our waists and higher. Some of the smaller campers had a genuine need for help from others near them. We walked as a total group with concern for the safety and feelings of each person. This was an authentic, stressful situation, and the cooperation and caring needed to bring everyone safely back to camp created a feeling of cohesiveness important to community building.

RULES

The co-directors of HRYAC developed a minimum list of rules they deemed necessary for the following: maintaining the health and safety of everyone; caring for equipment and the environment; and the perpetuation of the organization's good reputation in the eyes of both parents and the surrounding community. With these guidelines, a minimum set of rules was presented to the participants along with a reason or reasons for each rule. The consequences for breaking each rule were carefully outlined.

Many times, more rules did not have to be made beyond the minimum set until a problem arose that affected the community. A rule was most likely to be followed when everyone agreed with it. For this reason, additional rules were developed by consensus of the whole group. Reaching a consensus took time, but often resulted in greater cooperation with the rule. In reaching a consensus, everyone agreed that they would follow the rule, because it made sense to them.

Enforcing rules had to be consistent and direct. Community agreement on a rule made enforcing it much easier. The removal of privileges as a consequence for breaking a rule was more humane than any form of punishment, such as belittling or embarrassing the offender.

Respect for human dignity was the overriding guideline in making and enforcing rules. There are no simple answers to rule making and enforcing, but group discussion and problem-solving so that everyone wins was the goal. The use of power by those responsible for the program was inevitable, but it was kept to a minimum in order to realize the goals of self-discipline and mutual respect.

After much debate and hard thought, we arrived at the following list for our camp:
- Saws and knives are to be used only after adequate skill is demonstrated, because misuse of them may cause serious injury.
- The roof of the log cabin is off limits, because walking on the cedar shingles will break them.
- Fires are to be started only in the designated areas, because of the danger of fire in wooded areas.
- Shoes are to be worn at all times outside, because of the danger of cutting feet and the inconvenience of administering first aid.
- Participants are to sleep in their own tents, because of Health Department regulations concerning the number of individuals in each tent and the risk of damaging the reputation of the camp in the eyes of parents and others.
- Food consumption is for mealtimes only, except when a snack is served during the evening, because food quantities are purchased for meals and regular snacks only, and cleanup of utensils might be inadequate at any other times.
- Notify the staff if you leave the immediate camp area, because they are responsible for your health and safety at all times, and it is dangerous to be alone if an accident occurs.
- Don't wash with soap in the streams and lakes, because the pollution may destroy the living things in the water and make this area less attractive.
- Don't walk on the logs around the campfire circle, because they might roll, which can result in an injury.
- All accidents—major and minor—must be reported to the first aid person, because it is important to treat all injuries, and the staff may be liable for negligence if a problem arises in the future.

- Meat must not be put into the compost pile, because of the possibility of a dangerous animal coming into camp.
- No swimming is allowed unless a qualified water safety instructor is on duty, because of the danger of drowning.

Beyond these basic rules, campers had a wide range of choice in conducting their daily lives. It is always more difficult to extend a wide range of choices to campers, but the effort is worth it in building better decision-making skills. Unless campers feel they have a strong opportunity for input, they often will be unhappy and rebel. We did not expect the campers to always choose what we wanted for them, but as long as no rule was broken, we let them go.

All of us helped enforce the camp rules. It seemed like the power of a total community to enforce rules was much stronger than the power of any one person or small group.

Rules differ from the personal biases of the staff in that there are usually no major consequences to the offender when biases are ignored. Being in touch with personal biases, the opposite of value preferences, and distinguishing them from rules are important. Knowing that a behavior of a participant is bothersome, but is not against a rule, may influence how the leader acts toward the participant. The following section lists one author's personal biases when he conducts resident outdoor education programs.

14 PERSONAL BIASES (I WISH YOU WOULDN'T DO THESE)
(by Cliff Knapp)

- Tell "ghost" or other scary stories, especially at night.
- Tell "dirty jokes or stories," making suggestive sexual or gender references, or using off-color language.
- Permit verbal or nonverbal put-downs of others and yourself.
- Play traditional team sports (basketball, baseball, etc.) and other competitive games.
- Give material awards and prizes to a select few in games, contests, or daily-living activities.
- Permit any kind of littering or other kind of vandalism.
- Engage in "horseplay" or physical "roughhousing" with participants.
- Make threats that are unwise to carry out or administer physical punishments (e.g., pushups or running laps).
- Allow radios, TVs, stereos, music on cell phones, or computer screen use when they detract from the program activities.
- Permit yelling, screaming, foot stamping, booing, loud whistling, or other noises in inappropriate places.
- Permit inconsiderate noise and disturbance in cabins or tents after "lights out" time.

- Drink soda, eat candy, or have any special privileges in the presence of the participants.
- Ignore table manners, waste food, or allow contests that involve food or drink.
- Violate the rights of others as persons in any form (e.g., searching luggage or not respecting personal privacy).

What are your personal biases? Are they different from the rules you and your organization have established? Make a list of your personal biases and rules.

POSITIVE FOCUS

A primary goal for the three weeks of camp was to increase both self-respect and respect for others in the community. We wanted our campers to like themselves and others better by camp's end. A positive focus influenced nearly everything we did. A camp norm was a ban on "put-downs" and "killer statements"—actions and words that resulted in people feeling less self-esteem. Once the campers learned to recognize verbal and nonverbal put-downs, they cooperated by checking themselves and reminding each other to stop their negative actions.

A ritual that encouraged positive focus was called "new and goods." As part of each evening's program, we went around the circle, and staff and participants shared something that was new and good for them during the day. If someone could not come up with their own new and good, others were glad to help. Sometimes, we did a "proud whip," an activity in which each person completed the statement, "I am proud that ..."

We structured many occasions for giving and receiving compliments or validations. As part of the evening closing, we formed a five-minute validation circle in which anyone who had an appreciation for someone in the community could speak out and share it with the whole group. One problem that arose was holding the circle time to only five minutes each night because they loved to validate each other. Among other validation techniques were the following:
- *Validation envelopes*—Campers decorated envelopes with their names and artwork and hung them on the fireplace mantle. Scrap paper was left in a convenient place for use. Whenever campers wanted to share a positive comment, they wrote it on a piece of paper, signed it, and put it in that person's envelope.
- *Validation book*—Each person's name was written on a page in a notebook. The notebook was passed around, and positive comments were written on each page. At the end of camp session, campers were presented with their own page.
- *Focus person*—As a closing activity on the last night, each person had one minute when everyone in camp focused on them and showered them with validations. By limiting the time to one minute, they were left with the feeling that much more could have been said if the time had been longer.
- *Creativity night*—This is a time when individuals could get up in front of the group in an atmosphere of support and encouragement and share a talent. The sharing varied

from telling jokes, leading or singing songs, reading an original poem, or doing a skit. One boy, who was to have his Bar Mitzvah in the fall, shared some of the ceremonial chants. For some, it was easy; for others, it took great courage to perform in front of their friends. It was a time to focus on individuals. Both performers and the audience saw themselves and each other in new, positive ways. The applause following each performance was another way of giving nonverbal validations.

Focusing upon personal strengths was a theme that ran throughout the camp. One activity directed the campers to go outside and find something in nature that represented one of their positive qualities. When they returned, they shared their discoveries with one another. Self-concept building was an important aim, which we structured the program to accomplish.

TRUST-BUILDING

We believed that learning to appropriately touch each other to demonstrate friendship and caring was an important factor in building closeness and trust. With appropriate touch that respected other people's "space," we found that "getting in touch with others" (literally and figuratively) was a key component to building a safe community where people felt connected to one another.

We started with games such as "people to people." In this activity, the participants paired up and one person was chosen the leader. The leader called out the parts of the body the pairs must touch such as "toe to toe," "finger to finger," "arm to arm," or "knee to knee." When the leader called "people to people," everyone had to find a new partner. The person without a partner became the new leader.

Another touch activity involving a high level of trust was "people pass." This activity required from 16 to 20 people. After safety guidelines were clearly introduced, everyone stood together in a tight line with their arms raised. Each person, in turn, was then lifted, passed from the front to the back of the group, and gently lowered to the ground.

Massage was a popular activity. The campers divided into two groups. One group lay down on their stomachs with their eyes closed. The other group chose reclining partners, and under the leadership of a staff member, gave head, back, or foot massages. After a while, the groups switched roles. Gentle touching is a way to communicate caring, which, in turn, promotes trust. In any of these activities, as a way to respect other people's "space" and personal preferences, the option to pass, or not participate, was always honored without question (only a few individuals chose to exercise this opportunity).

Engaging in an activity called a "blind walk" was another way we built trust. The campers paired off, and one was blindfolded. The sighted campers guided their blindfolded partners, and nonverbally shared the environment with them through senses other than sight. Sometimes, the experience included a blind lunch. It took a high level of trust to allow the mutual feeding of an unknown meal.

Another technique for getting acquainted was small-group sharing. In this activity, we divided into groups of three or four and shared answers to questions such as, "What are some of the things I like about myself?", "What are my goals for the three weeks of camp?", "What will you like about me when you get to know me?", and "What fun things have I been doing this summer?" Because feeling listened-to is an important prerequisite to speaking freely, we used these small-group instances to introduce and practice listening skills. The act of listening with interest and caring while people talk about themselves is another method of promoting trust.

To let them know that we put a lot of trust in them, campers had considerable input and latitude in deciding how to spend their time. If two or three campers had something they wanted to do and could find a staff member to do it with them, it was generally done. Campers built and labeled their own nature trail, and constructed a tree house, a sauna and primitive shower, an underground fort, a raft, and a playground for toddlers complete with see-saw, birch-bark slide, and tire swing for the staff's young children. One group of campers and staff put on a circus for the whole camp. Another baked banana bread and made pizza for everyone. Everyone helped to cut down a giant dead birch that weighed hundreds of pounds. They hauled it several hundred feet, carved it with personal identity symbols, and erected it in place. It was such a highlight that we named the session, "The Year of the Totem." The campers also led their own activities for others to select. There was always an option to "do nothing" (if that's possible), but the offerings by staff and campers were so varied, that boredom and nonparticipation were not problems.

There were no skill awards for excellence following any of the activities. Everyone did their best and that was our measure of success. There were many cooperative projects that built upon different individual talents.

A 30-minute community meeting each night after dinner provided opportunities to solve problems and resolve conflicts. Any issues of concern in the community could be raised. To help the meeting organization, an agenda was posted all day, so that anyone could write an item down for discussion that night. Campers usually led the meeting and made sure that only one person spoke at a time. Everyone, including staff and directors, had to wait to be recognized by the leader before speaking. The community meeting was the foundation of much of the decision-making and was an important part of each day. When asked what they learned from community meetings, campers answered with three different types of responses:

- Most frequent were responses dealing with solving community problems. They recognized that problems can be dealt with openly and solved rationally by everyone.
- The next grouping of responses recognized how everybody's thoughts and opinions were considered and how people really cared about each other.
- The third grouping of responses dealt with speaking out and expressing thoughts and feelings in a large group of people.

These kinds of learning made the community meetings very worthwhile as another trust-building strategy.

PROBLEM-SOLVING

In any community, problems arise and need to be dealt with directly. We tried to include everyone in the discussions, decision-making, and coming up with solutions that could be accepted by everyone.

One technique to deal with an all-camp problem was fishbowling. This activity involved placing the whole group into two concentric circles. The inner circle discussed a topic for a period of time while the outer circle just observed and actively listened. Members of the outside circle were not allowed to interrupt. After a set time, the circles reversed, and the outer circle discussed the same topic.

This fishbowl technique was applied once when the staff became dissatisfied over picking up litter, equipment, and personal belongings of the campers. The staff went into the inner circle first and discussed their gripes about picking up after the campers. The campers listened intently, and when their turn came to talk, they expressed their feelings about the staff concerns. The whole group then divided into quarters to brainstorm ways of solving the problems uncovered in fishbowling. This was a morning activity for the whole camp and was very necessary to clear the air before doing other things that day. It took a lot of trust for each group to express concerns about the others and not fear punishment or rejection.

We dealt with problems as a community, and with a few exceptions, we allowed campers to influence camp policy. One time, staff-arranged groupings for an out-of-camp trip were challenged, and after considerable discussion, the decision was changed to allow the campers to group themselves.

At a community meeting, one girl broke into tears, because her tent was scheduled to be moved for an overnight trip. She was a long way from home and had been on the move all summer. After she expressed her feelings, it was easy to take another tent and give her the stability she needed. It took trust to speak out against the plan to take her tent, and it took trust to express feelings in the group.

In a primitive wilderness setting, daily living chores are obviously important to the successful functioning of the camp. If water is not brought up from the source, no one can wash. If dishwater is not put on the fire to boil well before the meal, everyone suffers, because dishes must be washed before other activities can begin.

The method for assigning responsibilities was decided by the campers. One year, a camper was appointed to design a caper or chores chart. Another year, people volunteered for jobs for the next day at the beginning of each community meeting. Campers were on their honor to volunteer for each job. Staff did not supervise all jobs, with the exception of cooking and dishwashing, which were health matters. Staff signed up for jobs, as did the campers. With no one telling them when to do their jobs, people had full responsibility to see that they were done. It took a lot of trust on the part of the staff to allow campers this freedom, and we found that when we extended trust in these areas, our faith was justified.

EVALUATION

The "Dear Me" letter was a technique that we found valuable for introspection and personal evaluation of the camp experience. This effort usually involved a self-addressed, private letter written by the campers to themselves. Subsequently, these letters were collected and mailed to each person a few months later. Sometimes, unfinished sentences were provided to give ideas for what to write about. The following are examples of excerpts from "Dear Me" letters written at HRYAC:

- "My favorite part of camp was the stream hike. Or maybe it was going to Montreal and singing on the sidewalk. There are so many great things about camp; it's hard to choose."
- "The low part of camp, I think, was when it was raining for about the fifth day. Everyone was restless."
- "I learned at camp that it's not something to be ashamed of to show your emotions."
- "I felt happy and loved here and like I really belonged."
- "I relearned macramé. It has been a fun part of camp."
- "I think the unique part of camp is that a group of so many people can be so close. There weren't any splits in the group."
- "I appreciate the community for accepting me and loving me and helping."

- "I learned how close people could really be. I felt close and related to everybody. I relearned how to be a better person. I am concerned about people here, and I only wonder whether I'll ever be this close to someone again."
- "I learned that there is a lot more love in the world than anyone thinks. I have also learned to care for people more and to hug and touch them … I appreciated myself for being part of the community and fitting in pretty well. I appreciated the community for including me and caring for me. See you soon."
- "I learned that I can be free with people and that they understand. I felt I have become a better person after I went to camp."
- "I need to know people want me and that I can show my love for them."
- "I appreciate myself for loving and caring for other people. I appreciate the community for being a great place to live for three weeks."

WE WANT TO KNOW

At the end of our three-week camp, we did a survey to find out just what type of impact we had on our campers. It was a sentence completion-type of questionnaire with 33 sentence stems:

End-of-Camp Survey

Our camp has come to an end for another year. What you take with you will be yours for the rest of your life. Please complete the following sentences. Feel free to add more to each sentence, if you wish.

- The best thing about the people at camp was …
- Living in the wilderness for three weeks was …
- The thing I enjoyed most about being here was …
- The thing that took the most courage for me was …
- One of the hardest things for me to do was …
- I did the following things for the first time in my life …
- One thing that helped me become more mature was …
- The most exciting thing that happened was …
- The scariest thing that happened was …
- One memory that I will keep for the rest of my life is …
- The people here who mean the most to me are …
- One thing I learned from the community meetings was …
- One thing I learned from the scheduled activities was …
- I got to know the people best when …

- The food was …
- If I were just starting this camp again today, I would …
- Sleeping in tents helped me feel …
- The counselors helped me most when they …
- The thing that bothered me most about camp was …
- If I had the power to make one change in this camp I would …
- Deciding what I wanted to do each day was …
- The jobs of cleanup, water, latrine, and cooking were …
- Nature is important to me because …
- The activity that was the most fun was …
- If I could return next year it would be because …
- One reason I wouldn't want to return next year is …
- This camp is different from most camps I know because …
- Some new activities I would add to the camp next year are …
- The best description of what happened at camp if anyone asks me is …
- The hardest decision I had to make was …
- Two words that best describe how I feel about camp are …
- The thing that I most want to say to Vera and Cliff (directors) is …
- Some other sentences I would like to write about the camp are …

The completions for the first sentence were very interesting because they revealed how the campers best got to know others in camp. Knowing people is part of trusting them. The answers fell into four main categories: one-to-one informal conversations; small group camp activities, such as trips, chores, or parties; responses to people having problems or being hurt; and whole-group trust activities, such as the stream walk, massages, or trust exercises.

A strong bond developed between many counselors and campers, and the glue was trust and respect. In response to the question asking when the counselors helped the campers most, the campers' responses fell into three main areas: verbal interactions, such as talking seriously, joking, encouraging, or comforting; conveying an attitude of respect, caring, or empathy by simply paying attention to them; and physical contact, such as backrubs, first aid care, trust exercises, or hugs. One camper said of counselor hugs, "It makes you feel really special, and no one is telling them to do it."

Only one response indicated that the counselor helped them most by teaching an outdoor skill. That activity was rappelling. That was a powerful finding to us. Our counselors were most helpful to campers when they were just there for them, talking to them, paying attention, or touching them. That finding indicates that time devoted to developing human relations skills paid off in building closer relationships.

Another question asking the campers to use two words that best described how they felt about camp demonstrated the importance of hiring a quality staff. Out of

23 different words used one year, just two words were used 13 times—"loving" and "caring." No other word was used more than twice to describe their camp experience. Among the other words used were togetherness, understanding, community, mature, nature, homesick, happy, fun, very free, great, and beautiful.

Something special must have happened to those who chose the words loving and caring. They felt strongly about who was there. When we asked the campers what they enjoyed most, over half mentioned the people.

HRYAC was an experiment in humanizing camping. Many of the program activities are repeated year after year because they "worked." New activities were tried each summer to continue our search for ways to promote an effective wilderness community in which good human relations, adventure, and a joy for living are the main goals.

SCHEDULE

Given the above component parts of HYRAC, how did we put all of the puzzle pieces together? What follows on pages 116 through 118 is a simple calendar of one three-week program to give you a sense of flow and an overview of the overall organization of the program.

EXCERPTS FROM THE DIRECTOR'S JOURNAL

What follows are excerpts from one of the director's journal and other writings by staff and campers to give you more of a taste for the camp, as well as a glimpse into the thoughts and feelings of a camp director.

- *August 3*—The question of why I'm running a camp for 24 kids faced me again tonight. Fatigue is probably the reason this question comes to mind. It seems like thousands of items are needed or wanted, and most of them have to be carried into the cabin one by one. This is hard work with pressures of great responsibility on my shoulders. Health problems have started already with Jay's sore throat and Judy's bee sting. Nothing serious yet.

  We ran one and one-half hours behind schedule due to a late bus pickup and heavy rains as the campers arrived. When the weather cleared, we congratulated ourselves on the success of the first day. It's tempting to tell the kids everything I think they should know to make our routines run more smoothly. It will take time, because they have to experience this themselves. Establishing a community of 40 or more is a big undertaking. The reasons I established this camp will undoubtedly become clearer as the weeks go by.

  Our problems seem to be with one girl who continuously holds her right hand to her mouth and says she has a toothache, a boy who is scared of other kids, and another kid who would rather be alone tonight in a tent. Another camper wants acceptance so badly that he attracts attention by his continuous wisecracks. What will tomorrow bring? Tonight will bring needed rest, I hope.

CALENDAR

*	Sunday	Monday	Tuesday	Wednesday	Thursday	Friday	Saturday
Morning		9 a.m. Nurse Check-In (Songs while you wait) Rules & Policies #2 Group Community Building (clock, line games, people pass, snail, cookie machine)	All Community Stream Walk	Guitar Chords Knife Safety/Saw Safety First Aid for Everybody Canoe Skills Weather Initiatives/Challenge Course Letters (Home)	Backpacking trip— Hike Cooking Raft Building Parachute Activity Miniature Golf Course	—— Raft Painting Frisbee Golf Sat. Dinner Planning Edibles & Blueberries Hike Candle Wax Melting	—— Happy Birthday Raft Painting II
* **Afternoon**	Arrival 4 p.m.- Community Meeting Teammate Selection Orientation to Camp Facilities	Fire Drill Tour of Camp (All) Swim Tests Canoe Tests Beach Activities	Validation Envelopes Skills Courses: First Aid, Knife Safety, Saw Safety	Hike to Reservoir Frisbee Golf Planning Optional Swim Synchronized Swim Swim Test Canoe Test	Singing Charades Cooking Mini-Hike Activity Nature Weaving	Wood Cutting and Raft Scraping Frisbee Course Body Painting Cookies & Dinner Macrame & Edibles Canoe Tests Utensils Dinner	New Games Natural Foods Dinner
* **Evening**	Meeting Rules & Policies #1 Getting to Know Each Other "New & Goods" Campfire Singing	New & Goods Calendar #2 Agenda "Getting to Know You" (Games)	Community Meeting Interviews #1	Name Drawing Interviews #2 Night Hike	Back Rub Introduction "New & Goods" Interviews #3	Barn Dance	Special Campfire

* Morning	Sunday	Monday	Tuesday	Wednesday	Thursday	Friday	Saturday
Morning	Hey, Hey, Hey What About Me? (Games)	Off Today (Anna B. & Sunshine) Raft Launching 10:30 Corn Bread Canoe Test Macrame Car Wash Raft & Service Creative Writing Knife & Saw Skills Drama	6:30 a.m. Early Bird Walk Blue Mt. Hike Lunch Pack Canoeing Woodcarving Macrame Song Writing Guitar Lessons Candle Making Drama	Laundry at Old Forge Guitar Lessons Bread Baking & Raspberry Hike Choc Cake Blueberry Picking Drama	Canoe Trip—— Hike & Nature Crafts, Beaver Sticks Tie Dyeing Prep. Drama Hike Creative Writing Pre-rappelling	——— Laundry at Old Forge Camp Empty: Inspector Inspects	——\ RAIN … Sleep, sleep … more sleep Branch Orifice Special Meal Committee
Afternoon	Hey, Hey, Hey What About Me? #2 New Games II Individual Time Rehearsal for Creativity Night	Pre-rappelling Candle Making Wild Rodeo Macrame/Cookies	2-4 p.m. New Games Sagamore Visit Happy Birthday Rehearsal for Creativity Night	2 p.m. Jam Making Cake Decorating Happy Birthday (Kara)	Tie Dyeing Swim 2 p.m. Frisbee Lessons, Ultimate Frisbee Nature Crafts and Sketches Cake Bake Road Crew Repair Pre-rappelling Lessons Happy Birthday, Dean!	Cookout on Beach Manhattan Comes Back! Inspector Inspects	Good Deed for the Day 2 p.m. Canoe Pickup Cooking Barn Busting Frisbee Tournament
Evening	Movie—Bless the Beasts and Children Group Interviews #3 Beasts Discussion	Mini-Canoe Trip #1 (Planning)	Mini-Canoe Trip Planning #2 Massage	Acid Rain People for Dinner Camp Interviews #4 Creativity Night	New Games Blob Tag Prui Killer Validation Circle Group Interviews #5	Magic Box "New & Goods"	50's Night

CALENDAR

*	Sunday	Monday	Tuesday	Wednesday	Thursday	Friday	Saturday
Morning	Backwards Sunday Newspaper Planning Tie Dyeing & Candles Nature Crafts & Gift Ideas Rappell Intro.	Backpack Trip #2 Run & Dip Group Interviews #7 Backpack II Hits the Trail Whistle Making Rappell Cookies Jell-O Community Newspaper Road	Expedition to a Secret Place Gifts Making Rappell Intro. Newspaper Planning	Frisbee Golf Opening Ceremonies Group Interviews #9 Gift Making Warm Fuzzing Writing Roadeo Shell Painting Rappell	Frisbee Tourney Newspaper Planning Oh Phi Hole Firewood Collecting Strengths Game Your Choice Help as Needed Drama	Last Night Planning Rappelling Breadmaking Newspaper Planning Initiatives A Bit O' Candles, Macrame and Lunch Drama	Kettle Circle Celebration Sierra Cup Ceremony Evaluations Dear Me Letters
Afternoon	Tie Dyeing & Candles Group Initiatives Swim Apple Luscious Making Hike for Nature Crafts Drama Crafts & Swim	Swim Large Candles Pre-Rappell New Games Cookies New Games Drama Lots of Fun— Group Initiatives	Return of Backpack II Return of Expedition Rappellers Return Many Happy Returns!	2 p.m. Acid Rain Lab Visit Swim Gift Making 4:30 p.m. Group Initiatives	Group Interviews #10 Sand City Options Massage Group Initiatives Newspaper Firewood Collection	Group Pictures Drama	Sad Hello Forevers! Depart for Home
Evening	Group Interviews #6 Vulture & Co. Story	Talkity Talk About Camp Tone	Group Interviews #8 Campfire	Celebration Night	8 p.m. Square Dance Fireside Watch All Night Vigil	Hambake Dinner Validation Circle	

Humanizing Outdoor and Environmental Education

- *August 4*—Larry conducted the "get-to-know" activities today. The pillow-throw game works quickly in learning names. I read a list of 12 camp rules to the group and posted them. Our first community meeting went well. Tomorrow, we plan a stream exploration and nature awareness session.

  The tent selections went smoothly. The campers decided on a system of requesting each of the nine tent sites in their group of three. If there was a conflict for a tent site, sticks of varying lengths were drawn to settle the conflict. Dawn, Jocie, and Beckie were the only ones who weren't satisfied with their site. Paul helped them pick a new place, and they re-pitched their tent.

- *August 5*—Today was the all-group stream hike. We drove them to where a stream crossed under a road and then walked downstream. It took about two hours at a slow, exploring pace. We waited for the tail end of the line every few minutes. We accomplished our purposes of nature awareness, adventure, and cooperation. We linked hands and arms and helped each other over slippery places and fallen logs. The winter wren, jewelweed, hornet's nest, crayfish, stoneflies, and the people in the group helped make the time enjoyable. Sometimes a simple activity is best.

  After the community meeting, we closed the evening with verbal appreciations for Paul and Kevin. We will do more each night. We need to pay attention to those who are quiet and hanging back. The group of campers from last summer and the new ones are blending into one community as the special magic of group building begins. The campers are speaking out openly and enjoying the freedom to be themselves. Apparently, the rules made sense, and they still know they have many choices in their lives.

  I wondered about confronting some of them with the issue of public display of affection. A few of the older campers paired off today to form couples. It is difficult to know when to raise my concerns and when to keep my doubts to myself. I wonder where that will go?

- *August 6*—The community meeting worked like the textbook says it should. Many people voiced their gripes and suggested solutions. We used the newsprint a lot for meeting agendas, notes of things to do, and the day-to-day schedule. We have only been able to plan the program one day ahead. There are still many things to do to make our home in the wilderness comfortable. For the first time, the mosquitoes are not overwhelming. Sue and Jenny took four campers on a night hike, and we were not bothered with noise around the campfire like the first night. A good staff, armed with lots of talent, dedication, and a work ethic, is surely the formula for success.

  I felt good today and now know why I'm running this camp. I get pleasure out of helping to make the world a better place. The Death of a Wombat story went over well tonight. Campfires and meetings seem to flow without strain. The campers love to sing, and Sue and Judy lead songs beautifully.

  The questions of swearing and going out on a group overnight without adult supervision were discussed and cleared up. Swearing and off-color jokes do make me uncomfortable. Also, going off in coed groups for an overnight is not allowed without staff being present. The campers did their Seton Watch (a time alone in the woods for reflection and quiet) today. I should have asked more of them for their reactions to this new experience. Some said they liked it. Others were not sure. We need to share the positive results of our day at meetings, rather than only deal with community problems.

- *August 7*—We need to plan the schedule a few days in advance to heighten the excitement for upcoming events and to show where we're going. Everyone seems happy with the way our lives unfold, day-by-day. This is a hard way to make a living, but my satisfactions are rewarding.

  After the community meeting, we had time for some contributions for a creativity night. We arrived at a consensus that our meeting would only last 30 minutes. I could have made that rule at the beginning, but it was better to have the whole group decide after a few evenings of long, drawn-out meetings. A rule will usually be followed when campers clearly see a need for it and respect the rule-makers. The need for the 30-minute meeting was clearly accepted and was held to.

- *August 8*—This morning, the participants created many useful and beautiful natural crafts, including a raft, a bench, a grass broom, a birch-bark basket, and a grass wall hanging. The beauty of the morning was that I was there to help get what was needed, and the campers did the rest. It was a good example of providing a rich environment and letting people do their "thing" (or allowing them to follow their creative urges). I was truly a facilitator and guide this morning, and not the boss calling all the shots.

  The community meeting went quickly, despite a large agenda. Our creativity night was a rousing success. There seemed to be true appreciation for all of the offerings. The next one will be even better, I predict. We closed the evening with everyone sharing their "new and goods" of the day. Finishing the birch-bark stitching, the good spirits of the group after realizing that they were lost, and the personal satisfaction about overcoming difficulties were some of the highlights of the day.

- *August 9*—This morning, we offered sessions in tree house, bench, and nature-trail building. The nature-trail activity didn't attract enough interest, but the others did. Instead of supervising the nature trail, I went with the creative writing group. It was another example of allowing things to happen, without standing in the way of creative, able staff. It also met my personal needs for creating and sharing. My guess is that all were happy this morning, because they chose what they wanted to do, and they had a hand in determining how to do it. I'm glad I decided to have this camp, because it reassures me that this is the right way to be a director.

  We had a long, but productive, community meeting, which got out a lot of feelings. We closed with "new and goods" and a birthday celebration for Ann. The group is molding rapidly into a cohesive, loving community. As our meeting went on beyond 9:30, I had to get away for a walk alone. I can only take so much of any group, before needing to get away. I have an ebb and flow of needs for group intimacy and to be alone.

- *August 10*—Today, the all-group trip to town to do the wash was undertaken. After deciding to take 15 campers in the morning and 15 in the afternoon, the campers didn't want to cooperate. Being together in certain groups was more important than the numbers we had picked to fit in the vehicles. Chaos sometimes reigns when free choice is given, but resentment may reign when campers are forced to do what they don't want to do. What is more important in solving this issue? I ask myself that question continuously about many things. It takes time to sort out the pros and cons involved in each decision made in a democratic community.

I went fishing alone today, and when I returned, everyone was involved in a massage activity. It is now "legal" to rub backs and necks and heads while the meeting is going on.

We closed the evening with a discussion of the upcoming camping trip. Some staff expressed concern about the formation of camper cliques. In private, they decided to break the clique up to force exposure to new people outside the clique. A clique shuts out others, and we agreed this was not fair to them. We didn't anticipate the effect of our decision on the campers when we told them about the new groupings for the trip.

The next item for discussion on the agenda was the splitting of the groups for the camping trip. Some of the members of the clique felt very close and knew that after the next few weeks, they may never all be together again. They couldn't accept our reasons for splitting them.

We had time to explore the feelings of some in the non-clique group too. They didn't seem to have any resentment about being excluded from the clique—at least no one expressed any. After the campers had a chance to express their feelings, I decided to let the campers regroup the way they wanted. The only ground rule was that the numbers should be even.

The meeting ended happily with the regrouping. The staff agreed to the regrouping when they saw how important it was for the clique group to stay together. Our plan to dictate the groupings for reasons of imagined or real hurts to the non-clique group didn't work. The issue was balanced almost equally between the pros and cons, so our change of plans was relatively easy.

One good thing coming from the meeting was the expression of feelings about cliques and their affects upon others in the community. We need more thought about when to structure the lives of campers and when to allow them free choices. Will being a camp director ever be an easy job?

- *August 11*—After an informal songfest, we had another community meeting. Some of the returning campers expressed how they thought the camp was stricter than the previous year. When is it acceptable to tighten the rules, and when should they be eased? We talked about the pros and cons of a "stricter" camp.

We ended the meeting with "new and goods" and a proud whip in which everyone mentioned one thing they were proud of about themselves. Dawn, Dean, and Jocie had difficulty in pinning down what they were proud about. Others in the group helped them when they couldn't think of something to say.

This community meeting structure provides a way for campers to ask for what they need. That's a useful life skill. There ought to be more ways to address different life skills in this setting. For example, we need to develop structured exercises for people to request and receive appreciations, find healthy alternatives for solving personal problems, search for better ways of using free time, and grow in empathy and other needs. What are more of our human needs and how can this community help in meeting these needs?

- *August 12*—This morning, we had a beautiful blindfold session. Starting with everyone blindfolded, we took paired journeys by tuning into our five senses. We did a tree fantasy in which we imagined we were small and could travel inside the vessels of a tree. We did a partner blind-trust walk. For the most part, it worked out better than I expected. The campers were really into the activities.

    To wind up the session before the blind lunch, most of the group played a game of passing natural objects in a circle, while blindfolded. We left the blind lunch optional, and most people decided to participate. Feeding someone or being fed were new experiences for most of them. My most persistent and powerful thought coming from the morning was that the campers, ranging in age from 11 to 14, had abilities and sensitivities that I usually expected only from adults. Are they really that different?

    Before the community meeting, the campers had a rousing soap foam fight. My only objection was the possibility of injury and the angry feelings that resulted in a few individuals. This "soap foam happening" provides a vivid example of the lack of consideration some had for others by forcing this messy game on them. If I had stopped the game at the start, this learning opportunity never would have been available to them. We have not come down as typical authoritarians in this wilderness community, but we do lead, guide, and organize. Very few things the campers do have made me angry.

    We give the campers opportunities to determine how they live their lives with us. We listen to them, help them solve problems, express our frustrations, and enjoy the benefits of community living.

- *August 13*—Our group living dynamics and community formation are going like an adult group's would. I'm beginning to doubt if there is a significant difference in human behavior, just because of chronological age. Campers seem to be able to ignore their chores more easily in preference to playing around. Maybe adults have been caught up in the work ethic and don't know how to play as well as young people do.

- *August 14*—Eve led a short community meeting tonight. Swearing was discussed in detail. The campers agreed to check out the group's preferences before swearing. If anyone in the group didn't feel comfortable with swearing, it wouldn't be done. That solution seems simple enough. I wonder if they can stick to that arrangement?

- *August 15*—The group that stayed back at camp decided to dig an underground shelter. I found a pick to make their digging easier. They'll cover the hole with boards and use it as a special retreat place. It's hard to do this back at their homes. Perhaps the biggest benefit they will get is a warm, close human interaction with each other. They stay close together and socialize in a tent after our meetings. I wonder how much they will take advantage of the beautiful Adirondack wilderness? Their social bonding need is strong at this age.

• *August 16*—Some campers are relaxing in the cabin, with books and letters, while others are improving the road, building a tree house, and making candles. Sue and Bob deliberately walked out on the tree-house group, because they believed they were taking charge too much. They thought by doing this, the campers could make more decisions on their own. My hope is that the safety aspect is maintained. I think I'll go check that out. After putting that extra spike in the tree, I can breathe easier now.

This afternoon, the staff expressed their concern over "helping" the campers too much. They thought they made too many decisions for them. They felt being sucked into a trap of "helping" and providing too many answers and too much structure. They decided to bring this concern to the meeting tonight. Sometimes they are confused about the staff's role in the community. They wonder how much they should lead compared to allowing the leadership to emerge from the campers.

Our goal is to gradually place more responsibility on them to help develop self-reliance. We want to share more of the leadership, but the weaning process is difficult. Maintaining control over their safety and health is important too. It's sometimes hard to know where and when to step in and where and when to step out.

• *August 17*—We went to Mt. Jo in the morning with all but two campers. The climb was steep, but we did it in less than one hour. On top, we made lunches and ate quietly. After lunch, we had 20 golden minutes of silence. I'm glad we required that 20 minutes, because some of the campers mentioned it as their "new and good" for the day. I forgot the topographic map of the area, but they enjoyed the views anyway. We stopped by the nature center for help with some local plant identification, but most of the campers wanted to hike.

We had problems with Kevin's acute littering habit. Nothing seemed to work. There must be better ways than telling him in front of the rest of the group, as well as privately. He must really care about the beauty of an un-littered environment. We can't force a love of beauty on him.

Darby led the community meeting. The campers freely shared some of the values that I have about living together and raised the same issues that I would have. I'm trying to maintain a low profile at the meetings and still get my concerns dealt with. Of course, I bring up topics that really bother me. The meetings are aimed at making our lives more rewarding.

• *August 18*—Writing this beside the stream is peaceful and relaxing. The rains came down hard after lunch. After a week of blue sky and warm sunny days, it just had to rain. The stream is high and churning beautiful black foam patterns in front of me. Occasionally, a fish feeds on the surface. A hummingbird just buzzed in to taste the jewelweed nectar.

• *August 19*—Inspired by "backwards day," a period in which the campers and staff did many things backwards all day, Stream wrote this poem, which may be read either forwards or sdrawkcab:

---

*Love of flowers
symbolizes love of life;
Breathing of fragrant winds
brings hope now,
recharging tired spirits,
strength returns again.
Low time contrasts with soaring,
touching inner caverns,
awakens knowing of strength within.*

*Flowers of love
life of love symbolizes;
Winds fragrant of breathing
now hope brings,
spirits tired, recharging,
again returns strength.
Soaring with contrasts, time low
caverns inner touching,
Within strength of knowing awakens.*

- *August 20*—Judy took my watch, and Sue made my lunch. They are clearly telling me this is my day off. I sorely needed it. There isn't enough time this summer to really enjoy a pressure-free Adirondacks romp. Hiking, fishing, and reading would feel good if I could find the time.

  Creativity night was fun. Trish and Jenny are leaving tomorrow, and we will be poorer for their going. I was presented with a validation sheet tonight—a long list of what the campers and staff appreciated in me. Love is growing in our community as time passes.

- *August 21*—We bid Jenny a tearful farewell. We talked about the value of crying when a few of the campers responded to her goodbye tears. Warm hugs arose naturally out of love and caring. This is a different kind of community, because of the frequent coming together and leaving each other, all in the course of three weeks. Saying tearful goodbyes will occur repeatedly in our lives. It feels good to provide support for this way of expressing sad emotions when someone special leaves. Hopefully, dealing with sad departures back home will be easier.

  I wanted to prevent the campers from taking too many blueberries home with them, while Vera thought that it was okay to pick as many as possible. I agreed to discuss the issue at the community meeting tonight. There was mixed reaction to my concerns. As a result, we decided to bring the question to a higher authority— the director of NHEC, our sponsoring organization. Since the director owned the land and the blueberries, it was his decision. We respected his decisions on this issue and it became clear that the power rests in different hands with different issues. He said it was okay to take the berries home.

- August 22—John spent the day with us and everyone loved his singing and guitar playing. When he was ready to go, I suggested that they express their thanks in nonverbal ways. It was good to see many campers hugged him, especially the boys. It feels good to encourage safe touching as a way to express caring. The "outside world" is often afraid to encourage touching as a form of human expression. Living together like this provides special opportunities that are hard to match in public schools. Why can't we find ways to spread what we have learned in this community to other settings? The dramas coming out of feelings of caring, sadness, anger, joy, and fear are real and important pathways for learning about our humanness in any setting.

- *August 23*—We had a terrific totem-raising ceremony. The campers changed their names and thought about changing a part of themselves too. We gained more insights into how the campers wanted to change.

This is my philosophy of camping: I believe that campers are persons with many of the same rights as adults. They deserve to be heard, to direct their lives in most areas, to speak out for what they want, as well against what they don't want, to structure most of their own time, and to share in the responsibilities of everyday living. Camp goals should focus upon growth about self and others and nature awareness and knowledge. Campers ought to be placed in environments that encourage decision-making and self-reliance whenever possible. Taking full responsibility is a gradual process and chances to do more should be increased daily.

Cooperation among all community members should be stressed. Competition in which bitter feelings result with only one winner and one loser should be underplayed and de-emphasized. Activities can be structured so that all people win. Rewards for excellence in skills should come from the pleasure and knowledge gained from doing the activity. Choice within a reasonable structure should be encouraged. The camp should be run like a democratic community—with all pulling together. Everyone contributes their talents to the tasks of living and growing together.

Child-like dependency patterns were gradually broken as the staff worked with the campers. Attention should be paid to how each person interacts with every other person. Putting this philosophy into practice is difficult and never fully finished. Understanding group dynamics and becoming more humane is a lifelong venture.

- *August 24*—This morning gave me time for myself. I am feeling less tense about "doing jobs," even if I don't feel like it. The community can almost run itself now. I don't feel that its success rests totally with me anymore. What a relief!

We are a close-knit community that came together to search for better ways of living. We try to face joys, as well as problems, head-on and experience them fully. We created a small society that takes the very best values from our larger society. We understand that we have the power to make a difference when we return to our homes. Since we live in the wilderness, each day brings new awareness and appreciation for nature. Because there is no electricity or running water, we work hard at the basics of living.

We have used the earth's gifts to make dye from plants, to find driftwood carved by lapping waters, to erect a giant totem, to make a tree house and underground shelter, and to eat from wild plants. We built a sauna, shower, rock drains, and nature trail. We felt the wind stroke our faces, heard the raindrops tap our tents,

---

and experienced the challenges of rappelling over a rocky cliff or carrying a loaded pack. The morning and evening chill helped us appreciate our warm sleeping bag more. Intimate encounters with the natural world are all around us.

We are continually involved in thinking about people-to-people interaction, which helps us grow. We are aware of our different values and interests, but, at the same time, celebrate what we have in common. We stress cooperation over competition, caring over contempt, and sharing over selfishness. We value trust in ourselves and in others. We focus upon what is new and good in our lives and on what we appreciate in others. Our goals are never easy, but we stretch ourselves every day. The one thing we know for sure, when it's time to return home, is that we know the rewards and problems of living together closely. We have attained a sense of community that so many others in the world hunger and strive for and never achieve.

A LETTER TO THE STAFF
(by Cliff Knapp)

Dear close friends,

Our Human Relations Youth Adventure Camp has been over for a week as I write this. I wanted to communicate my appreciation and reflect upon our accomplishments before the memories blur. Vera and I considered the camp a success, and we want to do it again next year. With every successful project, there are elements to improve. That thought is comforting, because it shows me that I've learned something and am growing in a good direction.

I would like to appreciate each of you for being you and for giving part of your life to an experiment in community building. It was an experiment and will always be that. Each time we do it, we will learn more and, in turn, will improve our approaches. As in any experiment, each discovery gives rise to new questions. Some of our hypotheses are confirmed, while others are tossed and replaced by new ones. Some experiments "work" and turn out the way we expected, and others don't.

We never experiment alone. We always build on the hard work and research findings of others. Some of our results are measurable, and some are not. We easily can count smiles, validations, and returning campers, but measuring happiness, caring, and self-esteem are not so easy. We can always learn more when we test our theories of improving human relations skills in this great experiment.

I appreciate each of you for being the trusting, loving, caring, happy, cooperative, understanding, real, honest, open, helpful, listening, and just plain nice persons you are. All of these adjectives describe you well. These words also came from the campers when they described the best things about our community.

We were an effective community, and we had more joy and hope for the future than in most communities I know. I appreciate you, because you cared enough about building our community and you devoted as much personal space as you could to that end. I know how difficult it was to give the space to a single goal. I appreciate you because you shared the good things in your lives with others. You spent your lifetimes getting ready and preparing for these times together.

I have often boasted, half-jokingly, that we have the longest staff training session of any camp in the world. You have trained for your lifetimes. I have also claimed, seriously, that we have one of the best camp staffs anywhere. You shared activities with others, because they were fun and beneficial to you in your life. You also responded to what the campers wanted to do if you saw that it was valuable and worthy of your precious time.

I appreciate you because you took active roles in improving our community when you thought your idea would work. I appreciate you also for your silence and patience when you thought what someone else tried wouldn't work. Sometimes, it's harder to do nothing and let things happen than to do something that inhibits a learning opportunity. I appreciate you, because you lived what we were trying to teach to the campers.

Our staff interaction was a microcosm of what we wanted to happen to the whole community. We expressed our thoughts and feelings, we cared about each other, and we worked hard at implementing a common goal. You gave permission to everyone else to live out the loving, understanding, and intelligent parts of us that are sometimes hidden beneath the armor of our back-home persona.

The list of appreciations would not be complete unless I appreciated myself, too. I appreciate my wisdom in gathering all of you and allowing you to be yourselves in all your magical manifestations. I appreciate how consciously I provided encouragement for you to practice the best skills you knew for building a solid community.

In addition, I appreciate my trust in everyone and the faith that we would succeed in taking the best from our outside world. I also knew that we would work hard to eliminate the worst from our larger society, such as verbal putdowns of ourselves and others, hatred, greed, violence, and all the other cancers that may emerge from living together closely. I appreciate myself for having the courage to make this camp a part of my life and to shoulder responsibilities involved with a community of this size. All of the difficulties in making our community work were outweighed by the tremendous gratification I received. Thank you for being part of my personal excitement in living out a dream.

I know that we will keep in touch throughout this year. Good luck in trying to spread the sense of community to the world around you now.

—See you on the trail,
   Cliff

IMPRESSIONS OF A NEW HRYAC CAMPER
(by Cliff Knapp, one year later)

The first day of camp finds me a little nervous inside. I wonder to myself, "What will happen next?" "How will I fit in?" "Who will become special to me?"

There is a friendly tone in the air and a sense of something different. Music and song smooth the way for learning more about the persons behind the faces. Gradually and magically, the caring sides of people emerge like caterpillars from chrysalises.

"What is happening to me?" I ask, pinching myself to see if I am dreaming. I feel better about myself in a way that's different. Can this be real?

I begin to see how I fit into our community. I marvel at my goodness and strengths. We are becoming less like isolated individuals and more like members of a close group. People really do care about me, and I care about them. This feeling is strange but nice.

You mean that I have a say in this community? I really have some power to make a difference here? It's scary to face up to knowing what happens to me is mostly my responsibility—that I can control much of my own life here. I feel like a fish trying out a new set of fins or a bird testing out new wings. I wonder where this will take me as I navigate toward my future.

The staff must trust me to make the right decisions. Wow, that is strange! What if I just wanted to sit in my tent all the time and play cards? Would they let me? Wait a minute; that would only hurt me! That is not what I came here for.

I want to know more about the wilderness and the people gathered around me. I want to try some new things and go different places. I want to be a bigger and better person when the time comes to leave. I want to do this to me and for me.

What can I give and what can I take? I want to keep the giving and taking in the right balance. What can I create with my own hands and brain?

How can I make the world a better place here and after I leave? How can I take more of this caring community and plant these seeds in the outside world? Can I do it alone? Where can I get help? Are people really different out there? Will I have to leave the sense of my own power in the Adirondacks?

No, I can find the caring sides of people everywhere. I can take this personal power with me when I leave. Yes, I have grown with the wilderness this summer and I will not stop now or ever.

Humanizing Outdoor and Environmental Education

HYRAC: WHAT IS IT?

(by Cliff Knapp, another year later)

Whenever people ask me to describe our camp, I have difficulty. The best way for them to understand what we are like is to live with us for three weeks. Since this is not always possible, I use words to paint pictures of HRYAC. I wonder if the words really do it? How can words describe feelings and experiences if another person has never known their meanings?

People also ask me what we do to create our sense of community. I whisper my secret formula: First, I invite the best people I know to join our staff. Then, I give them lots of room to be themselves and to do what they enjoy and do best. Then, I find a wilderness environment where we can live together. Then, campers join us who want to share outdoor adventure and improve their people and adventure skills. The last step is to give a great deal of mental and physical effort to make the community work. All of you know that fun, learning, and caring just don't magically appear in our lives. We plan specific kinds of activities to reach our goals.

The following are some of the words I use to describe HRYAC to others: Each year, I learn more about how to help our community reach some important goals. One goal is to become more trusting of others and be honest about expressing feelings. At the same time, I want to see people act in caring ways and be gentle with others. I want to see them recognize their strengths and to love themselves more. I want to see them become more in touch with their thoughts and feelings and be clearer about their values. I want to see them learn more skills of communication and use them to solve the problems of living together. I want people to feel a sense of community oneness and to work toward common purposes. Also, I want people to celebrate their differences and to respect others who are different. I want them to take more charge of their lives to get what they need and want.

HRYAC is based on the assumption that people will make the world a better place if they know how. The power of touch is used to communicate caring. Music is another tool for achieving some of the community-building goals. The daily community meeting is also an important part of solving the problems of living together. In this meeting, everyone is given the opportunity to be heard and to influence many decisions.

A great deal of freedom to decide how to spend each day is necessary for growth in self-responsibility. Self-confidence and clear direction in life result from opportunities for risk taking and self-stretching. Individual and group needs are both considered important.

These are some of the words I use to describe our camp. I know that they may fall short, because they don't have the same meanings to everyone. The true meanings are within each one of us. We know what HRYAC is, and no one can take our memories from us. We have lived together for three weeks. We have laughed, sung, hiked, swam,

---

touched, talked, cried, rejoiced, sweated, and felt hurt and anger together. We know what camp is. We can describe our camp to others by the special ways we live and interact with people. I know that the world is a better place for our being here and for spreading our community goals to others. Enjoy the adventure of living in your own separate communities and use some of what you have learned here.

THE ONGOING HRYAC EXPERIMENT
(by Cliff Knapp, another year later)

Some people may wonder why I still call our camp an experiment after so many years of operating. HRYAC will always be an experiment, no matter how long it continues.

Experiments are valuable ways of finding out new things. What we learn from experiments stays with us longer than if someone just told us about the results. Good experiments are conducted under suitable laboratory conditions. They follow intelligent guidelines and are based on accepted assumptions. Experiments attempt to answer important questions and give rise to others. An experiment well done requires skilled experimenters. Good experiments can involve mixing known substances in safe ways to avoid explosions or other accidents.

We are trying to find better ways of building a close, supportive community of people of all ages. We are striving to create a place for everyone to be somebody special. We want to create an atmosphere where people will have a sense of personal power to get what they need to live rewarding lives. We want people to like themselves more and to fill their time with worthwhile activities. We want them to express their thoughts and feelings easier in ways that consider others. We want them to be able to listen intently to others by "walking in their moccasins." Along with these human relations goals, we want people to love the natural environment and to work to improve the quality of life on earth.

What have we learned over these years? Occasionally, I am asked, "Does this kind of camp work?" My answer is clear, "Yes." In saying "yes," I know that we all take away different things in different amounts. Every year, we ask our community members to honestly tell us what they have gained in three weeks together. Even if some campers don't believe they have changed much, they say that they feel more loving, caring, trusting, important, and able to solve problems of living together. These changes don't always last when they go home, but some do. In general, they feel more in control of their lives and confident of their abilities. Most people agree that they have grown to be better than they thought they were before.

What are the conditions and guidelines under which all this happens? In order to grow, campers need the safety to make mistakes. Mistakes are viewed as good omens for growth. We strive to eliminate put-downs and name-calling. They also need recognition of their successes. We validate each other with words describing the strengths we see. We also support each other with lots of physical touch. We want our campers to feel the freedom to make decisions and to experience self-power.

We believe that expressing feelings of anger, joy, fear, and sadness are fine and normal. We encourage openness and attempt to deal with human conflicts directly. We have made other assumptions about people too. We believe that people are lovable and capable, that they are able to live together with people of different backgrounds. We assume that differences can be resolved satisfactorily without one winner and one loser emerging.

With a skilled staff that cares about creating a human-growing camp, we continue the HRYAC experiment. Our staff is the vital ingredient in our recipe. They help to create the norms that make our camp different. However, without the cooperation and commitment of our total community, our experiment would fail. We all know that our task is not easy and that there is always more to do. This is true of other types of experiments as well, so we continue our search for growth.

THE CAMPERS AND STAFF HAVE THE LAST WORD

It is appropriate that we end this chapter by letting the participants speak for themselves and their own experience in the Human Relations Youth Adventure Camp. What follows are excerpts from the HRYAC HOTLINES, our camp newspaper, spanning the years …

❑ Raft Painting:
"How about pink with elephant polka-dots?"

"Naw, I think a gigantic IALAC button in phosphorescent purple and green would be perfect."

"Could we each paint three-fifths of a board our own favorite color?"

And so, after careful deliberation and consultation among all concerned, we decided that the best decision would be to compromise and paint the raft a beautiful shade of stratocumulus grey. Mostly because it was the only shade of grey paint that we had.

Plus, it's Howie's raft. (Alan)

❑ Utensils Meal:
On Friday, August 4, at suppertime, everyone lined up to have tacos for supper, just as usual. Only one thing was different—we didn't use any forks or spoons. Instead, we used spatulas, potato mashers, strainers, soup ladles, huge spoons, peelers, and other strange kitchen utensils. Everyone seemed to have a good time trying to eat tacos and jello with our strange silverware. (Reenee)

❑ '50s Night:
The main attraction of the night was the '50s dance. All of the girls came in high ponytails, rolled up blue jeans, sweatshirts, and bobby socks. The guys came with white tee shirts, blue jeans, and, of course, slicked-back hair, loaded with hair goo. The music played was from '50s CDs, and everybody really had a lot of fun. Thanks to Boo,

Wendy, Peter, Maria, and Erika, the barn was in really good shape. Priscilla was there, of course, to chaperone, making sure there was no funny business.

Of course, we can't forget our live entertainment. Manhattan John made a special guest appearance. The crowd of teenage girls went wild and tried to tear at his clothes, but he kept cool and calm. He sang wonderful songs, and everybody was dancing and singing. Manhattan sang, and everybody danced and had a great time. It might have been the best '50s night in the history of HRYAC. I think it was. (Maria)

As I look into nature's mirror
after the rain I see the clouds,
the birds, the trees,
and someone's eyes looking back at me.

Who is this strange but familiar looking person?
Why is he in the mirror of nature?

As I look into the mirror I see the
feelings that lurk inside me.

Why does he feel the feelings I do?
Why does he think like I do?

The answer lies not in the mirror
but in his eyes. (Adidas)

❑ Saturnalia:

On Friday night, we had the first Saturnalia. Saturnalia is the Latin word for festivity or festival. It was more commonly known to the camp as the celebration of life. To start the celebration, we had previously picked people's names to make gifts for. We busily worked hard over beautiful gifts for two days.

On the festival night, the gifts were given and appreciated. Singing, laughing, and eating made it a real celebration. An evergreen tree in the cabin added a touch of festivity to the occasion. It was almost as good as Christmas. (A. A.)

❑ Thank You:

I came
alone, scared—anticipating what?
I was touched, cared for
Why? You hardly knew me
but you cared
I decided to try
I opened up a little

Humanizing Outdoor and Environmental Education

I shared a little
I was unsure. Am I doing all right?
You said, you're doing great, just fine.
I smiled. I like this
    being supported, feeling special a new feeling
It crept up on me
It was unexpected
    but I finally realized it. These weeks we spent together
    that feeling, a feeling of love I had never had before.
Thank you (Sandy B.)

❏ Rappelling:

Cliff's note: Although rappelling was named on the final evaluations as an activity that took the most courage, the scariest thing, and the hardest thing to do, Tom offers us another side of rappelling:

Rappelling with Sunshine, Boo, and Dean is very fun. You're entirely sure that they won't let you drop for very far. When you first go down, you're very nervous. But, the second time you go down, it's a snap. The beginner slope isn't anything, compared to the intermediate slope, although they both have hard parts to them. When you get to the bottom, you feel so proud of yourself for doing the rappel down that slope. (Tom)

❏ Earth Day:

EARTH DAY was a spectacular
experience. It was done in the
rain, which was very different
and very successful.
You heard and felt the rain hit
your face, as Elizabeth and Big
Ernie talked about the beauties
of nature and life. You had a
nice dream and clean feeling
after the showers. Everything
was sparkling. A dance of giving
gifts to trees was beautifully
portrayed by Elizabeth, Ann, Mitzi,
Jenny, Bev, and Sandy M. It was
fantastically done with creative movement.

THE WILDERNESS WONDERS
drama troupe pantomimed Hope
for the Flowers by Trina
Paulus. The troupe included Scott,
Chris, Mitzi, Wayne, Becky, and Eve.
Thanks, Elizabeth, for a neat idea.
(Eve Knapp)

Where are all the stars?
The stars have fallen to the ground
There's not a star around

The earth is source-full
It gives life to many things
Mud forms when it rains
The plants and flowers float away
The sun comes back again. (Mitzi)

❑   My Spot:

I have a spot
I call my own
It is a place where
I can be alone
I love my spot, I do
It's my spot
*   my own. (Jodie)*

❑   You Mean So Much to Me:

Of all the people that make up
the world, I love you the most.
Nowhere do your smiles dominate
the environment—like they do in
this community.
I look at you, and I see—I feel love
You touch me with so much care
When you sing to me, my being
overflows with happiness.
And most of all you share your-
self with me—
All of you—you mean so much to me.
I love you so. (Big Ernie)

He rises majestically over his people,
allowing wind to sway his arms to and fro,
He is King.
His back is bent from time,
gnawed from wind and rain.
His figure silhouetted against the
*   Starry sky shows his wisdom.*
He is the mighty pine tree. (July)

❑ My Back Rubs:

When I feel the need to have a backrub, I just come up to someone and say, "Would you please give me a backrub?" They usually say, "Sure." Then, I lay down on my stomach and relax. Then, they give me a soothing backrub. Occasionally, a couple of "just a little bit up mores" or "a little to the lefts" come out. When someone comes up to me and says they need a backrub, I do the same. I sooth their muscles and scratch their mosquito bites. I try to give them a backrub they will never forget! (Kara Cutbill)

❑ Climbing a Mountain, Mirror of Life:

*"How many flights of stairs in an apartment building does this
mountain equal?" "We figured we would walk 190 blocks if we were
in the city." "Are we at the top yet?" "I can't go any farther."
"Let's count steps to see how many we can go before we rest again ..."
When you approach a high peak hike, Phelps Mt.—4161 ft., what appears
to be a hill to climb becomes a battle between mind and body. The
way you decide to solve this adventure, oftentimes, reflects the
ways you handle other life situations.*

❑ You Bring Your Self to the Mountain:

*You make the decisions when to rest, and when
to go, and how to hold on.
        You make sure your footing is steady,
your hands embrace the bark of a tree's trunk
for support.
        You are on your own and yet together.
        Another's hand reaches out, contact,
and then letting go.
        Where do you need to stop for yourself?
Is it the mountain's summit?
WE ALL WENT HIGHER ... (Bev Lazar)*

❑ Why Do We Have to Go?

*It is so peaceful here, where the rivers flow,
so why do we have to go back?
Being in touch with nature,
learning with the trees,
so why do we have to go?
Sweetness is in the air,
times are changing, we are growing,
so many problems, we can solve them here.
Look around at your friends,
people who love you so
So why oh why do we have to go? (Erika)*

> *"The child's impulses are an enormously important educational resource, and opportunities should be provided for children to develop them through engagement in activities."*
>
> —John Dewey

REFERENCES

The Human Relations Youth Adventure Camp included hundreds of active learning and interactive learning activities that focused on nature and human nature. To get a taste for these activities, be sure to refer to our companion book, *201 Nature and Human Nature Activities*, which is described at the beginning of the Resources chapter in this book.

CHAPTER 10
CAN I QUOTE YOU ON THAT?: QUENCHING QUEST FOR QUINTESSENTIAL QUOTABLE QUOTATIONS

"Quotationality defines us. We are what we quote."

—Gary Saul Morson

We have provided you with food-for-thought quotations at the beginning and end of each chapter in this book and its companion book, *201 Nature and Human Nature Activities*. Just in case you haven't met your quota of quotable quotations yet, the following are 25 more that you can add to your repertoire. You may want to think about how the words of others can stimulate your ideas. These words may either reinforce some beliefs that you hold dear to your heart or cause new, but related, ideas to suddenly "pop" into your head. We follow these quotations with some thought-provoking questions off which you can hop, skip, springboard, and somersault.

- "In the end, the ancient precept 'know thyself' and the modern precept 'study nature' become at last one maxim."

    —Ralph Waldo Emerson

- "You are richer today if you have laughed often, given something, forgiven more, made a new friend, have taken time to trace the wonder of Nature in the commonplace things of life."

    —David Grayson

- "Now I see the secret of making the best persons: it is to grow in the open air and to eat and sleep with the earth."

    —Walt Whitman

- "It is not enough to insist upon the necessity of experience, nor even of activity in experience. Everything depends upon the *quality* of the experience which is had."

    —John Dewey

- "By ethical conduct toward all creatures, we enter into a spiritual relationship with the universe."

    —Albert Schweitzer

- "Authorities generally agree that outside of schooled settings, children acquire skills through observation and participation in the contexts in which these skills are customarily invoked."

    —Howard Gardner

- "Those who dwell among the beauties and mysteries of the earth are never alone or weary of life."

    —Rachel Carson

- "You do not learn by doing . . . you learn by thinking – acting – thinking – acting, etc. In and of itself, doing, like experiencing, can be a mindless affair."

    —Seymour B. Sarason

- "The only kind of learning which significantly influences behavior is self-discovered or self-appropriated learning – truth that has been assimilated in experience."

  —Carl Rogers

- "The way we harm the earth affects all people, and how we treat one another is reflected in how we treat the earth."

  —Paul Hawken

- "Only through emotion do we know thee, Nature! We lean upon thy breast, and feel its pulses vibrate to our own."

  —Margaret Fuller Ossoli

- "Concern for this Earth community must itself bring about a deeper sense of the community of peoples upon the Earth."

  —Thomas Berry

- "The world is made up by us, out of our experiences and the concepts we create to link them together."

  —Otto Fritsch

- "Land ecology discards at the outset the fallacious notion that the wild community is one thing, the human community another."

  —Aldo Leopold

- "We can never speak of nature without, at the same time, speaking about ourselves."

  —Fritjof Capra

- "What we know of ourselves 'inside' is ultimately what we will allow ourselves to know of nature 'outside,' for nature is also us."

  —Theodore Roszak

- "I only went for a walk and finally concluded to stay out till sundown, for going out I found I was really going in."

  —John Muir

- "As scientific understanding has grown, so our world has become dehumanized. Man feels himself isolated in the cosmos, because he is no longer involved in nature and has lost his emotional 'unconscious identity' with natural phenomena."

  —Carl G. Jung

- "UNESCO identified and advanced four pillars of learning: learning to know, learning to do, learning to be, and learning to live together."

  —Stephanie Pace Marshall

- "Those who are really awake to the sights and sounds which the procession of the months offers them find endless entertainment and instruction. Yet there are great multitudes who are present at as many as threescore and ten performances, without ever really looking at the scenery, or listening to the music, or observing the chief actors."

  —Oliver Wendell Holmes

- "This new definition [of quality of life] must . . . include a sense of oneness with the total community of earth, which encompasses the human community in posterity and distance as well as presence. This requires humaneness and must be regarded as a part of the challenge of environmental education."

  —John C. Miles

- "The world is getting too small for both an *Us* and a *Them*. *Us* and *Them* have become codependent, intertwined, fixed to one another. We have no separate fates, but are bound together in one. And our fear of one another is the only thing capable of our undoing."

  —Sam Killermann

- "If you understand what makes a people laugh, you are closer to understanding and appreciating them."

  —Joseph Bruchac

- "Like a welcome summer rain, humor may suddenly cleanse and cool the Earth, the air, and you."

  —Langston Hughes

- "Nature doesn't move in a straight line, and as part of nature, neither do we."

  —Gloria Steinem

QUOTABLE QUOTATIONS QUESTIONS

- Which quotations most closely reflect your philosophy of teaching and learning?
- Which quotations suggest activities related to connecting nature and human nature?
- Which quotations are helpful in putting your philosophy of humanizing education into a few words?
- Are there any quotations with which you disagree?
- Which quotations best express your feelings about nature?
- Which quotations best express your feelings about human nature?
- Based on the aforementioned quotations, which quote-giver would you like to know more about as a person?
- What quotations that resonate with you will you add to this list?

Humanizing Outdoor and Environmental Education

If you want to find more quotations on the Internet or in books or articles, there are plenty to be found. Quotations can capture your thoughts or feelings in ways that seem to be just right. You may also want to write your own. Maybe what you write will become well known and others will use your quotation to express what they experience in nature and human nature. Don't be afraid of becoming addicted to collecting quotations. You can quote us on that!

> *"I really didn't say everything I said."*
>
> —Yogi Berra

Humanizing Outdoor and Environmental Education

CHAPTER 11

RESOURCES: WHERE DO YOU GO FROM HERE?

Wavebreakmedia Ltd/Wavebreak Media/Thinkstock

"In the case of good books, the point is not to see how many of them you can get through, but rather how many can get through to you."

—Mortimer Adler

You have gotten through our book to this point, and we hope that our book has gotten through to you as well. We want to leave you with some great next steps and additional resources to springboard off this book. This includes many recent resources, along with classics that we are calling "Oldies *and* Goodies" (marked with an *). We are providing you with more than 125 annotated suggestions for a variety of great books, periodicals, websites, and organizations that you can tap in humanizing outdoor and environmental education. First up, be sure to check out our companion book described as follows:

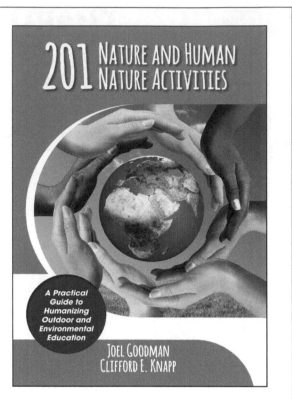

❑ Goodman, Joel & Knapp, Clifford E. (2017). *201 Nature and Human Nature Activities*. Monterey, California: Healthy Learning.

> This companion book springboards off the foundation laid by the book you are holding in your hands. It contains a gazillion time-tested ways (give or take a couple quadrillion) to put into practice the thought-full ideas underlying the current volume. You will find oodles of engaging, enjoyable, entertaining, encouraging, enticing, educational exercises, exploring the connection between nature and human nature. With a balance of outdoor and indoor invitations to connect with the natural environment and to connect with others, you will find a treasure trove of individual, small-group, and large-group activities, along with guidelines concerning how participants can get the most out of these activities. You will discover practical humanistic education strategies to help people of all ages in schools, camps, youth groups, religious institutions, YMCAs, adult education, families, and other settings, to promote mindfulness, awareness, and respect for nature and the environment; to develop communication skills; to build a sense of community; to clarify personal, social, and environmental values; and to nurture self-esteem. As icing on the cake, this book will leave you laughing… and thinking… about important environmental issues through John McPherson's internationally-syndicated *Close to Home* cartoons.

BOOKS

❏ *Abram, David. (1996). *The spell of the sensuous: Perception and language in a more-than-human world.* New York: Vintage Books.

The author, an ecologist and philosopher, writes for everyone who loves nature and human nature. He states: "The simple premise of this book is that we are human only in contact, and conviviality, with what is not human."

❏ *Ackerman, Diane. (1991). *A natural history of the senses.* New York: Vintage Books.

The beginning sentence—"How sense-luscious the world is"—sets the stage for a detailed look at the senses of smell, touch, taste, hearing, vision and then how "synesthesia"—a rare ability to combine several senses and blend them together—occurs. The author believes that the human mind is not in the brain as much as it is in the senses. A must for understanding sensory awareness and mindfulness.

❏ Aldo Leopold Foundation. (2016). *Leopold education project: Interdisciplinary land ethic curriculum.* Baraboo, WI: The Aldo Leopold Foundation.

The book presents a helpful collection of 20 middle and high school lessons, based on Leopold's classic, A Sand County Almanac. Activities focus on indoor and outdoor observation, participation, and reflection. Describes Leopold's land ethic and offers additional resources, including 28 outdoor exploration cards.

❏ Bentley, Michael L., Mueller, Michael P., & Martin, Bruce. (Eds.). (2014). *Connecting children to nature.* Bethany, OK: Wood 'N' Barnes Publishing.

The book offers a broad overview of what some describe as the "New Nature Movement." Twenty-five authors contribute chapters, which are divided into five sections: why it matters; developing empathy; exploring local natural environments; change through social action, and resources. Includes 35 activities throughout the book.

❏ Bourne, Barbara. (Ed.). (2000). *Taking inquiry outdoors: Reading, writing, and science beyond the classroom walls.* Portland, ME: Stenhouse Publishers.

The book features a collection of 10 chapters by participants and staff about inquiry into nature's treasures. A byproduct of a National Science Foundation-funded program (Elementary Science Integration Project) linking science to reading, writing, and other curricular areas. An excellent Resources chapter takes you deeper into this exploration.

❏ Broda, Herbert W. (2007). *Schoolyard-enhanced learning.* Portland, ME: Stenhouse Publishers.

The book is a practical guide for those wanting to use local outdoor places for teaching awareness to nature and the built environment. Based on extensive experience in the field and classroom teacher input, the author gives a gift to place-based educators. The appendix contains several useful resource links.

❑ *Caduto, Michael J. & Bruchac, Joseph. (1988/1997). *Keepers of the earth: Native American stories and environmental activities for children.* Golden, CO: Fulcrum, Inc.

A classic bestseller that combines the authors' talents as storytellers and educators. Chapters on storytelling tips and original stories from several tribal nations, such as Abenaki, Onondaga, Navajo, Nisqually, Lakota, Yurok, and many others, each followed by activities related to wind and weather, water, sky, seasons, plants and animals, and other nature and human nature topics.

❑ Cain, Jim, Cummings, Michelle, & Stanchfield, Jennifer. (2005). *A teachable moment: A facilitator's guide to activities for processing, debriefing, reviewing and reflection.* Dubuque, IA: Kendall/Hunt Publishing Company.

The book is a helpful guide to leaders, featuring over 120 field-tested activities and useful suggestions for implementing and reflecting upon them. These authors have a lot to say about how to help participants get the most from their joyful experiences.

❑ Cain, Jim & Smith, Tom. (2007). *The revised & expanded book of raccoon circles: A facilitator's guide to building unity, community, connection and teamwork through active learning.* Dubuque, IA: Kendall/Hunt Publishing.

The subtitle of this publication describes this book perfectly. It is a useful resource for humanizing adventure-based learning.

❑ *Canfield, Jack & Wells, Harold. (1976/1994 2nd ed.). *One hundred ways to enhance self-concept in the classroom.* Englewood Cliffs, NJ: Prentice-Hall.

This book features loads of strategies for teachers, parents, and other youth leaders who are interested in knowing how to enhance self-concept. Drawn from values clarification, magic circle, effectiveness training, and achievement motivation, this pioneering book in the field of self-esteem offers a goldmine of practical activities, which are still valuable today.

❑ Charles, Cheryl & Samples, Bob. (2004). *Coming home: Community, creativity and consciousness.* Chicago, IL: Personhood Press.

This book focuses on how to create environments in which individuals feel productive and fulfilled. Strategies for tapping into one's creative potential resulting in greater balance in family, business, school, social, and civic settings. Topics include the power of words, metaphor, natural guides to community building, learning styles, intercultural learning, core personalities, and ways to reduce stress and prejudice.

❑ Cohen, Michael J. (2007). *Reconnecting with nature: Finding wellness through restoring your bond with the earth.* Lakeville, MN: Ecopress, Finney Publishing.

For many years, Dr. Cohen has conducted nature-connecting experiences for participants in his workshops and courses. He developed a great number of powerful sensory-awareness activities to capitalize on a natural attraction humans have for nature. He proposes that humans have 54 senses.

❑ *Cornell, Joseph. (1979). *Sharing Nature with Children*. Nevada City, CA: Ananda Publications.

A classic collection of 42 games that are designed to connect nature with children and adults, in a way that expands their awareness of nature and human nature. The games are divided into several categories, including calm/reflective, active/observational, and energetic/playful. Revised and expanded in 2015 (see below).

❑ *_____. (1989). *Sharing the Joy of Nature: Nature Activities for All Ages*. Nevada City, CA: Dawn Publications.

Later re-titled, *Sharing Nature with Children II*, this book is filled with an explanation of flow learning and 19 activities.

❑ *_____. (1998). *Sharing Nature with Children*, 20th Anniversary edition, Nevada City, CA: Dawn Publications.

This book is a revised and expanded version of the classic parents' and teachers' nature awareness guidebook that was first published in 1979 and which contains over 50 activities.

❑ _____. (2014). *The Sky and Earth Touched Me*. Nevada City, CA: Crystal Clarity Publishers.

A book of nature awareness activities divided into three parts. Part #1 contains 11 exercises, designed primarily for individuals. Part #2 contains seven exercises to do with friends. Part #3 contains exercises to commune with life and live in oneness. Concludes with additional resources.

❑ _____. (2014). *Listening to Nature: How to Deepen Your Awareness of Nature*. Nevada City, CA: Crystal Clarity Publishers.

Extensively rewritten from the original book, this book offers adults a guide to deep awareness of nature through awareness techniques. Beautiful photographs and quotations from famous naturalists extend the book's value.

❑ _____. (2015). *Sharing Nature: Nature Awareness Activities for All Ages*. Nevada City: CA: Crystal Clarity Publishers.

After selling more than half a million copies, this classic has been rewritten and expanded with new activities and games, combining two previously published books by the author into one.

❑ Cross, Aerial. (2012). *Nature sparks: Connecting children's learning to the natural world*. St. Paul, MN: Redleaf Press.

A book designed to help preschool and kindergarten teachers plan and implement nature-based experiences. Four chapters and appendices offer numerous ideas for curriculum and instruction enrichment.

❑ *Dewey, John. (1963). *Experience and Education*. New York: Collier Books.

John Dewey, one of the most influential American philosophers, specialized in education. In this relatively short book, he describes a theory that forms his philosophy of education. A "must read" to better understand the founding father of experiential learning.

❑ Egan, Kieran, Cant, Annabella, & Judson, Gillian. (Eds.). (2014). *Wonder-full education: The centrality of wonder in teaching and learning across the curriculum*. New York/London: Routledge Taylor & Francis Group.

This book offers philosophical and practical chapters, integrating wonder into the curriculum to evoke a sense of wonder in participants. In three parts, the authors explore the educational uses of wonder, the method of wonder in classrooms, and the dimensions of educational wonder as they encourage teachers to realize that wonder lies at the heart of learning.

❑ Fleischman, Paul. (2014). *Eyes wide open: Going behind the environmental headlines*. Somerville, MA: Candlewick Press.

This book is designed to give teenagers an in-depth look at the complexities of climate change and other current environmental issues. Divided into six parts: noticing; perception; defense mechanisms; systems; attitudes; and eyes abroad and ahead. Useful resources are listed.

❑ Frank, Laurie S. (2001). *The caring classroom: Using adventure to create community in the classroom and beyond.* Madison, WI: GOAL Consulting.

This book provides an excellent overview of the adventure education field and how to integrate some of its ideas into the curriculum. Also useful also for camps, churches, and other youth organizations. Helpful list of resources included. See her website, GOAL Consulting, for more recent editions of this and other books. www.goalconsulting.org.

❑ *Gardner, Howard. (1999). *Intelligence reframed: Multiple intelligences for the 21st century.* New York: Basic Books.

Gardner follows his earlier books on multiple intelligences with this one and adds two new types of intelligences to the original list of seven—existential and naturalist intelligence. He describes how his ideas evolved and were revised. Important information to understand a holistic approach to working with youth and adults.

❑ *Glashagel, Jerry, Johnson, Mick & Phipps, Bob. (1976). *Digging in … Tools for value education in camping (camp director's handbook and camp counselor's handbook)*. New York: National Board of YMCA.

This publication uses the values clarification approach to help camp counselors clarify their own values and begin to build a valuing environment for campers. These books contain many practical suggestions for implementing a values education program in camps. Strategies are provided for mealtimes, campfires, hikes and nature study, sports, etc.

❑ *Goleman, Daniel. (1995). *Emotional intelligence*. New York: Bantam Books.

This book provides an overview of the ability to show zeal and persistence, and to control and motivate oneself. Guides readers to scientific insights related to emotions—how to understand them and how to bring intelligence to emotion as the end goal.

❑ _____. (2006). *Social intelligence: The new science of human relationships*. New York: Bantam Books.

Written as a companion to *Emotional Intelligence*, the book focuses on human interaction and answers important questions about relationships. Reveals findings from the field of social neuroscience in areas such as accurately empathizing, listening, knowing the social world, interacting nonverbally, and caring about others.

❑ Goleman, Daniel & Senge, Peter. (2014). *The triple focus: A new approach to education*. Florence, MA: More Than Sound.

A 92-page book about social emotional learning and systems education and their value in teaching today's youth. Emphasizes three core skills—understanding self, others, and the larger social systems. Examples from research and modern educational programs using these skills are highlighted.

❑ Goodman, Joel. (1995). *Laffirmations: 1,001 ways to add humor to your life and work*. Deerfield Beach, FL: Health Communications, Inc.

Joel believes that "Seven days without laughter make one weak." With this in mind, he delivers 52 weeks of ideas on how to increase your H.Q. (Humor Quotient). Each day of the year includes a thought-provoking quote (some of which appear in this book) along with action-inviting, practical humor tips to help you get more smileage out of your life and work. With this timely and timeless book, you will be grinning from year to year! Available through HUMOResources online bookstore at https://www.humorproject.com/humoresources/productdetail.php?product=101.

❑ *Goodman, Joel (editor). (1978). *Turning points: New developments, new directions in values clarification, volume I*. Saratoga Springs, NY: Creative Resources Press.

This book contains a stimulating and varied collection of 20 articles by leaders in the field, who explore the very latest thinking on values clarification theory and practice. This volume explores the applications of values clarification to education, families, business, youth organizations, and trainers/consultants. It also contains sections on new practical strategies, questions and answers about values clarification, and annotated resource lists.

❑ *_____. (1979). *Turning points: New developments, new directions in values clarification, volume II*. Saratoga Springs, NY: Creative Resources Press.

There were so many good contributions to the first volume that a second volume was published in response to popular demand. Like Volume I, this book has sections on innovations in theory and practice, new strategies, and resources in the field. It includes descriptions of how to apply the values clarification approach to a wide variety of fields and helping professionals.

❑ *Goodman, Joel & Furman, Irv. (1981). *Magic and the educated rabbit: A handbook for teachers, parents, and helping professionals*. Paoli, PA: Instructo/McGraw-Hill.

This book features a collection of easy-to-do and powerful magic tricks. What is unique about this book is that the authors describe hundreds of ways of using the tricks to address important learning objectives (e.g., using magic as an aid to learning subject matter, creating a positive learning environment, helping young people learn such life skills as observing, communicating, enhancing self-esteem, etc.).

❑ *Goodman, Joel & Huggins, Ken. (1981). *Let the buyer be aware: A practical handbook for consumers, teachers, and parents.* La Mesa, CA: The Wright Group.

This compelling book includes hundreds of practical activities and ideas for taking charge of your lifestyle; making sense of important consumer issues; developing life skills; helping students to become more effective consumers and citizens; and applying the values clarification approach to consumer education. The authors also provide a powerful curriculum-development model, which teachers and parents can use to generate millions of ideas for classroom lessons and family discussions.

❑ *Gordon, Thomas, with Burch, Noel. (1974/2003 by Penguin, Random House) *Teacher effectiveness*. New York: David McKay.

This book discusses how to apply important communication skills of parent effectiveness training, such as I messages, active listening, and no-lose problem-solving to schools, camps, and other youth organizations.

❑ Greenaway, Roger, Bogdan, Vaida, & Calin, Iepure. (2015). *Reviewing: A practical guide for trainers and facilitators.* Charleston, SC: Bogdan Vaida.

This book presents a very thorough treatment of the reviewing or reflecting step in facilitating the learning process. The authors have extensive experience in helping participants make meaning from their experiences. The book provides practical tips for making the reviews highly engaging and valuable. See Chapter 6 in the book you are holding for an insightful interview with Roger Greenaway. For more on Roger's work, visit http://www.reviewing.co.uk/.

❑ *Harmin, Merrill, Kirschenbaum, Howard, & Simon, Sidney. (1973). *Clarifying values through subject matter.* Minneapolis: Winston Press.

The book features many suggestions for using values clarification in various subject areas. Especially useful for camps and resident outdoor education centers is a chapter describing 15 values strategies in environmental education.

❑ Hawken, Paul. (2007). *Blessed unrest: How the largest movement in the world came into being and why no one saw it coming.* New York: Viking.

The book looks at the results of a survey of North America's environmental and social justice groups, devoted to protecting and healing a degrading planet. It describes the participants' aims and ideals in a movement that arose to address environmental and human ecology issues. Hawken estimates that there are over one million groups dedicated to this end. See his www.wiserearth.com website for more information.

❑ Hirsch, Jude & Priest, Simon. (2004). *Essential elements of experiential programming*. Published by TARRAK Technologies (North Adelaide, South Australia).

This book and others, which are available on the website www.simonpriest.altervista. org/TRRK, is designed to assist leaders in enhancing experiential programming training for those wanting more information. It includes resources, terminology definitions, models, and case studies.

❑ Humberstone, Barbara, Prince, Heather, & Henderson, Karla A. (Eds.). (2016). *Routledge international handbook of outdoor studies.* London/New York: Routledge Taylor & Francis Group.

This 529-page "encyclopedia" of multidisciplinary information in the broad field of outdoor studies covers most everything an outdoor leader would want to know. Identifies important issues, key research, philosophical approaches, and practical suggestions for conducting a wide range of outdoor programs. The most comprehensive book ever published on the topic.

❑ *Johnson, David & Johnson, Roger. (1975/1998 5th ed. by Pearson) *Learning together and alone.* Englewood Cliffs, NJ: Prentice-Hall.

This book is a classic in the field of cooperative education. The book provides numerous learning activities to maximize the attainment of cognitive and affective goals. The authors' theory is grounded in research and practical experience with youth.

❑ Kahn, Peter H. Jr. & Kellert, Stephen R. (eds.). (2002). *Children and nature: Psychological, sociocultural, and evolutionary investigations.* Cambridge, MA: MIT Press.

This book features a collection of thought-provoking chapters answering many questions about children and their connections to nature. Educators will find support for programs that seek to increase opportunities for children to relate to their environment in satisfying ways. The list of contributors includes some of the most competent people researching this topic today.

❑ Kimmerer, Robin W. (2013). *Braiding sweetgrass: Indigenous wisdom, scientific knowledge, and the teachings of plants.* Minneapolis, MN: Milkweed Editions.

The author, a professor and botanist of Potawatomi heritage, weaves indigenous wisdom and native science together by relating personal stories of her life in rural New York. Reveals insight into how land-based people use plants and how scientists view them. Readers will gain greater skills and understandings of ecology.

❑ *Kirschenbaum, Howard. (1995). *100 ways to enhance values and morality in schools and youth settings*. Boston, MA: Allyn and Bacon.

The author describes this book as "a comprehensive approach to values education and moral education." Surveys the field and offers one hundred different methods for teaching values and morality. Anyone working with youth will benefit from the insights of this values education expert.

❑ *Knapp, Clifford E. (1988). *Creating humane climates outdoors: A people skills primer*. Charleston, WV: ERIC Clearinghouse on Rural Education and Small Schools and Appalachia Educational Laboratory.

This book points out suggestions and activities for creating humane climate outdoors, including building intentional communities, teaching intrapersonal skills (becoming aware of feelings; affirming personal worth; demonstrating humor and imagination; recognizing personal power; and others), and interpersonal skills (communicating thoughts/feeling; empathizing; interpreting nonverbal language; questioning; validating others; and others). Includes an annotated bibliography, as well as an interview with Sue Flory, former Human Relations Youth Adventure Camp director.

❑ *_____. (1992). *Lasting lessons: A teacher's guide to reflecting on experience*. Charleston, WV: ERIC Clearinghouse on Rural Education and Small Schools and Appalachia Educational Laboratory.

One of the early books for experiential educators, designed to help with skills of reflecting/reviewing. Covers educational theory, practical leadership issues, questioning techniques, and alternative strategies to facilitate groups. Still available on the Internet.

❑ *_____. (1996). *Just beyond the classroom: Community adventures for interdisciplinary learning*. Charleston, WV: ERIC Clearinghouse on Rural Education and Small Schools.

This book contains background of educational reforms through outdoor education, planning for out-of-school lessons, and outlines for 12 outdoor adventure themes. Eight appendices provide additional aids for implementing lessons. Many activities can be taught in the city, as well as in rural areas.

❑ *_____. (1999). *In accord with nature*. Charleston, WV: ERIC Clearinghouse on Rural Education and Small Schools and Appalachia Educational Laboratory.

The subtitle, "helping students form an environmental ethic using outdoor experience and reflection," describes the purpose of the book. Filled with many ideas for conducting lessons about the threatened quality of the environment. Values and ethics resources and a bibliography direct the reader to other places for assistance.

❑ Knapp, Clifford E. & Goodman, Joel. (1981). *Humanizing environmental education: A guide for leading nature and human nature activities.* Martinsville, IN: American Camping Association.

This book is the original classic that has now been revised and expanded in 2017 into two books: *Humanizing Outdoor and Environmental Education* (the book you are now holding) and *201 Nature and Human Nature Activities*.

❑ Knapp, Clifford E. & Smith, Thomas E. (Eds.). (2005). *Exploring the power of solo, silence, and solitude*. Boulder, CO: Association for Experiential Education.

This book offers a compilation of 22 chapters from an eclectic group of university educators, clergy, and experiential education consultants and instructors. The book is divided into four parts: theoretical frameworks; research results; leadership in action; and personal perspectives. Appendices include a dialogue with the editors, quotations about the solo experience, activities for individuals on solos, and an epilogue.

❑ *Leopold, Aldo. (1949). *A sand county almanac and sketches here and there*. London/Oxford/New York: Oxford University Press.

A classic read for all nature leaders by one of the most famous wildlife biologist/ philosophers of the 20th century. Part #1 contains essays about nature around his Wisconsin shack through the calendar year. Part #2 features essays from various parts of the country. Part #3 offers essays about environmental esthetics and ethics. The book is designed to be helpful in learning about reading the landscape and developing a personal philosophy.

❑ *Leslie, Clare W., Tallmadge, John, & Wessels, Tom. (1999). *Into the field: A guide to locally focused teaching*. Great Barrington, MA: The Orion Society.

Insights about teaching about your surroundings by four talented naturalists (including an introduction by Ann Zwinger). Includes awareness activities through writing and reading on the landscape. Includes many useful resources for preparing natural leaders.

❑ Loh, Wan Inn & Jacobs, George. (2003). *Nurturing the naturalist intelligence*. San Clemente, CA: Kagan Publishing.

A collection of 150 nature-related lessons for students in grades 3 to 8. Organized into nine units, each focusing on key questions, such as "Why are pollinators our lifeline?" and "What are you eating?" Contains the tools teachers need to help children develop their naturalist intelligence.

❑ Louv, Richard. (2008). *Last child in the woods: Saving our children from nature-deficit disorder*. Chapel Hill, NC: Algonquin Books.

First published in 2005, this book was one of the catalysts that gave rise to the "New Nature Movement"—the rebirth of interest in providing youth with deeper connections to nature. Recognizes the societal issue of diminishing nature experiences (nature-deficit disorder), due largely to urbanization and increasing technologies. Filled with information about the need for nature contacts. Provides a compelling argument that action should be taken to correct a critical problem.

❏ _____. (2011). *The nature principle: Human restoration and the end of nature-deficit disorder*. Chapel Hill, NC: Algonquin Books.

This principled book states that a "reconnection to the natural world is fundamental to human health, well-being, spirit, and survival." Calling for a better balance between "screen" time and direct experiences in nature, Louv directs his argument towards adults. Backed by research, anecdotes, and follow-up resources justifying this call to action, he presents a convincing case.

❏ _____. (2016). *Vitamin N: The essential guide to a nature-rich life.* Chapel Hill, NC: Algonquin Books.

In the third book in his trilogy, Louv concentrates on practical suggestions for enjoying and benefiting from nature experience. Filled with project ideas, individuals in schools, families, and other institutions will be able to spend many hours outdoors healing the growing disconnection to nature.

❏ Martin-Schramm, James B., Spencer, Daniel T., & Stivers, Laura A. (2015). *Earth ethics: A case method approach.* Maryknoll, NY: Orbis Books.

Using the case method approach to study the earth's contemporary issues, the authors demonstrate the ethical dimensions of real dilemmas, addressing such issues as population, food, genetic engineering, water rights, coal removal, fracking, nuclear waste, urban growth, and free trade. Also provides resources for teaching.

❏ Meier, Daniel R. & Sisk-Hilton, Stephanie. (Eds.). *(2013). Nature education with young children.* New York/London: Routledge Taylor & Francis Group.

This book is a collection of chapters by 11 authors about teaching nature to young children. Combines theory and practice, based on inquiry approaches to learning. Research and background for early childhood educators wanting to implement a curriculum.

❏ Moore, Kathleen. D. & Nelson, Michael P. (eds.). (2010). *Moral ground: Ethical action for a planet in peril.* San Antonio, TX: Trinity University Press.

This book provides an overview of a survey of society's moral foundation and a call to action to do the right thing to heal a threatened planet. Some of the best minds in the world respond to the question: "Do we have a moral obligation to take action to protect the future of a planet in peril?" This question is answered from different perspectives, including survival, children, all life on earth, human virtue, gratitude, reciprocity, stewardship, compassion, justice, and more.

❏ Orr, David. W. (2004). *Earth in mind: On education, environment, and the human prospect*. Washington, D.C.: Island Press.

This book features essays that address many aspects of the societal need for improved education for the environment. This 10th anniversary edition is divided into four sections: dealing with the problem of education; first principles; rethinking education; and destinations for the future. A must-read for individuals interested in background on humanizing environmental education.

❏ *Purkey, William. (1970). *Self-Concept and school achievement.* Englewood Cliffs: Prentice-Hall.

This classic gives educators and parents an excellent grounding in the importance of self-concept in education. It explores theories of self-concept, documents powerful research findings, focuses on the direct relationship between self-concept and success, and suggests some practical implications for the teacher.

❏ *Raths, Louis, Harmin, Merrill, and Simon, Sidney. (1978). *Values and teaching: Revised edition.* Englewood Cliffs, NJ: Prentice-Hall.

The groundbreaking, classic book in values clarification includes a discussion of theoretical issues and research resulting from years of applying the theory in schools, camps, and other institutions. Provides the foundation for the principles and practice of values clarification. The book features numerous strategies to help youth clarify important issues in their lives.

❏ *Read, Donald, Simon, Sidney, & Goodman, Joel. (1977). *Health education: The search for values.* Englewood Cliffs: Prentice Hall.

This book presents new developments in how the values clarification approach is defined, along with new applications to the field of health education. The authors present dozens of practical activities focusing on such content areas as human sexuality, drug abuse, and nutrition, while simultaneously showing how these exercises can be used to develop valuing skills. The book includes an innovative chapter on humanistic approaches to evaluation.

❏ *Read, Donald & Simon, Sidney (ed.). (1975). *Humanistic education sourcebook.* Englewood Cliffs, NJ: Prentice-Hall.

This book is filled with scores of essays by leading figures in the early humanistic education field. Half of the essays deal with theoretical issues, while the other half focus on specific techniques for applying the philosophy with youth.

❏ Rinehart, Kurt. (2006). *Naturalist's guide to observing nature.* New York/Harrisburg, PA: Stackpole Books (now National Book Network).

This book is a guide to North American birds, mammals, and plants that is designed to help naturalists get to know nature through a natural history/ecological approach. Of particular value is the information included concerning how individuals of all ages, especially students in grade 7 and up, can identify these items in the field.

❏ Rivkin, Mary with Schein, Deborah. (2014). *The great outdoors: Advocating for natural spaces for young children.* Washington, D.C.: National Association for the Education of Young Children.

A revised and expanded edition of an earlier book, this volume cites research and program examples to help convince educators that young children need nature play for their full development.

❑ Robb, Marina, Mew, Victoria, & Richardson, Anna. (2015). *Learning with nature: A how-to guide to inspiring children through outdoor games and activities.* Cambridge, UK: Green Books.

A compilation of 97 field-tested activities and games for children and youth of all ages. Divided into four themes: games; naturalist activities; seasonal activities; and survival skills. Useful tips and photos are included.

❑ *Rogers, Carl & Freiberg, H. Jerome. (1994). *Freedom to learn: A view of what education might become, 3rd edition*. New York: Pearson.

Rogers, one of the founders of humanistic psychology, offers a well-tested philosophy of human growth and development. He believed that people grow through being genuine, caring, and empathic, as well as through congruent interaction with others.

❑ *Rohnke, Karl. (1984). *Silver bullets: A guide to initiative problems, adventure games, stunts and trust activities.* Dubuque, IA: Kendall/Hunt Publishing Company.

This book is full of activity ideas for building a sense of community. These games, trust exercises, initiatives, and stunts (activities that never grow old) come from the creative mind of Karl Rohnke and his work at Project Adventure.

❑ *_____. (1989). *Cowstails and cobras II: A guide to games, initiatives, ropes courses, & adventure curriculum.* Dubuque, IA: Kendall/Hunt Publishing Company.

Rohnke is a world leader in the field of adventure education. The book takes readers through the steps needed to become skilled in conducting camp and recreation programs. Includes useful curriculum models for camps and schools at all levels, based on actual working programs.

❑ Rosenberg, Marshall B. (2003). *Nonviolent communication: A language of life.* Encinitas, CA: Puddle Dancer Press.

Nonviolent communication is a process of communicating with compassion and empathy. The process has four components: observations, feelings, needs, and requests. An important book concerning how to maintain civil relationships and effective communities.

❑ _____. (2012). *Living nonviolent communication: Practical tools to connect and communicate skillfully in every situation.* Boulder, CO: Sounds True.

The book features chapters on the use of nonviolent communication in a variety of situations, such as conflict resolution, extraordinary relationships, healing and reconciliation, beyond anger management, parenting, and practical spirituality.

❑ *Roszak, Theodore. (1992). *The voice of the earth.* New York: Simon and Schuster.

In order to fully understand ideas about nature and human nature, the reader should understand ecopsychology. Roszak states that the goal of this book "is to bridge our culture's long-standing, historical gulf between the psychological and the ecological, to see the needs of the planet and the person as a continuum." It includes a list of ecopsychology principles.

❑ Sanborn, Jane & Rundle, Elizabeth. (2011). *101 Nature activities for kids.* Monterey, CA: Healthy Learning.

A compilation of 101 wonderful nature activities field-tested at Sanborn Western Camps and High Trails Outdoor Education Center in Colorado. The activities are easy to access and arranged under seven categories: sensory awareness, sense of wonder, natural concepts, scavenger hunts, along the trail, night, and art.

❑ *Satir, Virginia. (1990). *Peoplemaking.* London: Souvenir Press.

First published in 1972, this classic was originally written for parents by a family therapist. The contents are useful for anyone who is interested in developing better communication and self-esteem. Many of the techniques are still applicable today.

❑ Schoel, Jim & Maizell, Richard. (2002). *Exploring islands of healing: New perspectives on adventure based counseling.* Beverly, MA: Project Adventure, Inc. and J. Weston Walch.

A useful combination of adventure and counseling, the book includes theory, assessment, activities, and debriefing aids. Field-tested by Project Adventure, the contents are designed to help leaders conduct programs that heal participants' physical, cognitive, and emotional selves.

❑ *Sergovanni, Thomas J. (1994). *Building community in schools.* San Francisco, CA: Jossey-Bass Publishers.

The book offers a theory of authentic community building directed mainly at principals and teachers. The underlying concept, however, applies to leaders in all fields. Describes types of communities, the need for community, becoming a purposeful community, and leadership ideas.

❑ *Simon, Sidney. (1973). *I am lovable and capable.* Niles, IL: Argus Communications.

The IALAC story demonstrates what can happen to a person's self-concept in a typical day. Simon suggests ways of using the story for leading discussions and conducting activities. We included an adaptation of this insightful story at the beginning of Chapter 1 in this book.

❑ *_____. (1978). *Negative Criticism.* Niles, IL: Argus Communications.

This book follows up on the IALAC story (see Chapter 1) by exploring the effects of criticism on self-concept. The author also looks at what we can do to stop putting each other down, and how to appreciate ourselves and one another more. As with his previous book, Simon does this in a colorful, creative way.

❑ *Simon, Sidney, Howe, Leland, & Kirschenbaum, Howard. (1978). *Values clarification: A handbook of practical strategies for teachers and students: Revised edition.* New York: Hart Publishing.

This publication is a very extensive activity book on values clarification, featuring descriptions of over 2,000 examples of 79 distinct strategies. These strategies cover a wide variety of values-rich topics. This best-selling book is a goldmine that propelled the field of values clarification.

❑ Simpson, Steven, Miller, Dan, & Bocher, Buzz. (2006). *The processing pinnacle: An educator's guide to better processing*. Oklahoma City, OK: Wood 'N' Barnes Publishing.

One of several books written in the 21st century to help experiential educators facilitate reflecting and reviewing (an effort that is referred to as processing) sessions. The authors present helpful information by proposing an instructional model, sample activities, a facilitator's field guide, and references for further study.

❑ Smith, Thomas E. & Knapp, Clifford E. (Eds.). (2011). *Sourcebook of experiential education: Key thinkers and their contributions.* New York/London: Routledge Taylor & Francis Group.

The book has four parts that cover educational philosophers/theorists; nature study, outdoor and environmental education; psychologists/sociologists; and school/program founders. Readers learn about who influenced today's leaders of experiential nature and human nature programs and curricula.

❑ Smith, Tom & Allison, Pete. (2006). *Outdoor experiential leadership: Scenarios describing incidents, dilemmas, and opportunities.* Lake Geneva, WI and Tulsa, OK: Raccoon Institute Publications and Learning Unlimited Publications.

The book addresses situations in which leaders must make decisions about the health, safety, and learning of the participants. The publication is particularly helpful as a staff development tool to provoke discussions on proper judgment. Numerous comments and advice follow from seasoned experiential educators.

❑ Sobel, David. (2004). *Place-Based education: Connecting classrooms & communities.* Great Barrington, MA: The Orion Society.

The book is an invaluable primer on place-based education by one of the leading experts in the field. It is filled with helpful hints and follow-up resources. Sobel's book, Children's Special Places, Beyond Ecophobia, and Mapmaking with Children, is also an exceptional resource.

❑ Stanchfield, Jennifer. (2016). *Tips and tools for the art of experiential group facilitation (2nd Ed.).* Bethany, OK: Wood 'N' Barnes Publishing.

The book offers a practical tool for learning and teaching about experiential facilitation written by a practitioner who has a strong background in the philosophy of experiential education.

❑ Turkle, Sherry. (2011). *Alone together: Why we expect more from technology and less from each other.* New York: Basic Books.

Outdoor leaders should know something about the impact of recently developed technologies on people. Turkle, a psychologist, studied this impact and enlightens readers about the topic in this book. The growing "nature-deficit disorder" results from these recent societal innovations.

❑ *Van Matre, Steve. (1972). *Acclimatization: A sensory and conceptual approach to ecological involvement.* Martinsville, IN: American Camping Association.

A classic book that originated in a camp setting and was subsequently adapted for schools and other institutions. Van Matre broke ground for others who followed, with nature immersion and sensory activities, combined with group-process techniques, such as role-playing, communication skills, and fishbowling.

❑ *_____. (1972). *Acclimatizing: A personal and reflective approach to a natural relationship.* Martinsville, IN: American Camping Association.

A follow-up to Acclimatization, this book includes several sensory exercises and techniques, such as quiet walk, environmental study station and trail, Crusoe camp, Muir trek, Seton journey, and Walden solo. Each of these immersion experiences is accompanied by separate activities and leader guidelines.

❑ *_____. (1979). *Sunship earth: An acclimatization program for outdoor learning.* Martinsville, IN: American Camping Association.

The book presents a complete five-day program for understanding how the world functions. Ecology and human relations activities include cognitive and affective learning. See also Earthkeepers (1988) and Sunship III (1997), written by Steve Van Matre with Bruce Johnson.

❑ *Vinal, William G. (1963). *Nature recreation: Group guidance for the out-of-doors.* New York: Dover Publications.

Originally published in 1940, the book is loaded with ideas for teaching about nature. Vinal, one of the most renowned pioneering naturalists of the early 20th Century, gives readers ideas about the philosophy and applications of nature recreation. A valuable classic.

❑ Warden, Claire. (2012). *Nature kindergartens and forest schools.* Perthshire, Scotland: Mindstretchers Ltd.

The book describes a nature kindergarten in Scotland and others around the globe. Uses case studies from learning centers to assist formal and non-formal schools, as well as families, to use local environments with young children.

❑ *Weinstein, Matt & Goodman, Joel. (1980). *Playfair: Everybody's guide to noncompetitive play.* San Luis Obispo, CA: Impact Publishers.

The classic in the field of cooperative play. It includes a lively look at why we should be serious about play, along with 60 fun, highly participatory games, exercises, and icebreakers used around the world that invite cooperation, inclusion, and self-esteem. The activities are designed to build people up and bring people together in schools, camps, colleges, conferences, families, meetings, and corporate events. The book features unique and insightful chapters on how to lead and facilitate playful experiences and how you can create a million of your own positive, noncompetitive activities.

❑   Wilson, Edward O. (2016). *Half-earth: Our planet's fight for life.* New York/London: Liveright Publishing Corporation.

The third book in Wilson's trilogy of warnings about the Earth's threats to environmental quality. He proposes setting aside half of the Earth's places as reserves in order to maintain biodiversity and the ecological services. Read all three for a full picture of the state of the planet's health.

❑   Wilson, Ruth. (2012). *Nature and young children.* New York/London: Routledge Taylor & Francis Group.

A 118-page guide to establishing early childhood nature programs and playscapes. Includes ways to evaluate playspace, adult-child interactions, and academic integrity.

❑   Woods, Annie. (2016). *Elemental play and outdoor learning.* New York: Routledge Taylor & Francis.

This book combines well-established ideas and theories of outdoor play experiences and connects them to spiritual development in children. Addresses holistic development, exploratory and social skills, and imaginative play with natural materials.

❑   Young, Jon, Haas, Ellen, & McGown, Evan. (2008). *Coyote's guide to connecting with nature for kids of all ages and their mentors.* Shelton, WA: OWLink Media.

This book is essential reading for nature leaders. Young and his associates at the Wilderness Awareness School are skilled practitioners, as well as deep thinkers of nature philosophy. A rich source of activities and for digging deeper into indigenous and living-close-to-the-land ways.

PERIODICALS

❑   *Green Teacher: Education for Planet Earth* is published quarterly. P. O. Box 452, Niagara Falls, NY 14304-0452 or 95 Robert St. Toronto, ON M5S 2K5. www. greenteacher.com. One of the best and most practical periodicals covering all aspects of nature and the environment education.

❑   *Journal of Adventure Education and Outdoor Learning.* An international journal based in the United Kingdom and first published in 2000 under the auspices of the Institute for Outdoor Learning. www.outdoor - learning.org.

❑   *Journal of Experiential Education.* A collection of academic research, articles, and reviews, showcasing experiential education. The official journal of the Association for Experiential Education. www.aee.org.

❑   *Journal of Outdoor and Environmental Education.* An international journal published twice a year and devoted to sharing empirical and non-empirical articles. Owned by the Outdoor Council of Australia. www.outdooreducationaustralia.org.

❑   *Journal of Outdoor Recreation, Education, and Leadership.* (Sagamore Publishing) Devoted to improving the field of outdoor education through articles on professional practice, research, and theoretical discussion. www.ejorel.com.

❑ *Laughing Matters.* Free, bi-monthly email newsletter published by Joel Goodman and The HUMOR Project. Includes humor tips, quotes, cartoons, anecdotes, and the latest in the humor field. Designed for anyone who believes in humoristic education and wants to tap the positive power of humor in everyday life and work. Sign up by emailing info@HumorProject.com, with "Humanizing/Humorizing" in the subject line.

❑ *National Wildlife and Ranger Rick.* Designed for various ages 0 - 7+, the magazine is dedicated to protecting wildlife and habitat and inspiring conservationists. www.nwf.org.

❑ *Orion Magazine.* Explores the connection between nature and culture, and inspires thinking about living justly, sustainably, and joyously. A premier magazine for nature lovers and activists. www.orionmagazine.org.

❑ *Taproot Journal.* Dedicated to communication for the enhancement of education in the outdoors. A journal of the Coalition for Education in the Outdoors, a network of organizations and other institutions promoting education in, for, and about the outdoors. www.outdooredcoalition.org. Department of Recreation, Parks, and Leisure Studies, SUNY at Cortland, Cortland New York. Published from 1995 to 2015. The group continues to publish *Research in Outdoor Education.*

❑ *The Leopold Outlook.* Published by the Aldo Leopold Foundation's Land Ethic Press and dedicated to the Foundation's mission of fostering a land ethic through the legacy of Aldo Leopold. P. O. Box 77, Baraboo, WI 53913 mail@aldoleopold.org.

ORGANIZATIONS/CONSULTING SERVICES

❑ Alfie Kohn's written materials are located at www.alfiekohn.org. He has written numerous books and articles over the years containing important insights into humanizing education.

❑ Association for Experiential Education. AEE seeks to connect the global community of educators and practitioners and to expand their capacity to enrich lives through experiential education. www.aee.org.

❑ Center for Nonviolent Communication, founded by Marshall B. Rosenberg. This nonprofit peacemaking organization is devoted to meeting everyone's needs through nonviolent communication. www.cnvc.org.

❑ *Close to Home.* John McPherson's syndicated cartoon that appears in 700+ newspapers worldwide. John not only has published over 20 book collections of his cartoons, he also has an award-winning line of greeting cards, a yearly block calendar, and numerous other licensed products. John is part of The HUMOR Project's speakers bureau and been an active speaker for organizations, schools, associations, hospitals, and human service agencies around the country. To contact John about speaking, email info@HumorProject.com. To get a taste every day for more of his cartoons that will invite you to laugh and think, visit http://www.gocomics.com/closetohome.

❑ Collaborative for Academic, Social, and Emotional Learning (CASEL). The mission of CASEL is to make evidence-based social and emotional learning (SEL) an integral part of education, from preschool through high school through the use of five core competencies: self-awareness; self-management; responsible decision-making; relationship skills; and social awareness. www.casel.org.

❑ David Suzuki Foundation is devoted to protecting the diversity of nature and our quality of life through education and information. 219 – 2211 W. 4th Ave, Vancouver, BC Canada V6K 4S2. www.davidsuzuki.org.

❑ Earth Kin. A consulting organization headed by Wanda Dewaard in Walland, TN. Her programs encourage self and Earth awareness, celebration, kinship, and hope. www.earthkinship.com. Email: earthkin@bellsouth.net.

❑ Experiential Tools. A consulting organization headed by Jennifer Stanchfield and devoted to providing resources for cooperative and experiential programs. www.experientaltools.com. Email: jen@experientialtools.com.

❑ High Five Adventure Learning Center. Specializes in adventure program trainings and symposia. It is a rich source of information and assistance in experiential programming. Located at 130 Austine Dr. Ste. 170, Brattleboro, VT 05301. http://www.high5adventure.org/. Email: info@high5adventure.org.

❑ Kohler Experiential Learning Center. 444 Highland Dr. MS036 Kohler, WI 53044. Teambuilding consulting in adventure, problem-solving, assessments, and leadership. www.kohlerlearningcenter.com. Email: Kelc@Kohler.com.

❑ Nature Explore Program. Collaboration between Dimensions Educational Research Foundation and the Arbor Day Foundation to promote nature and culture connections. www.natureexplore.org

❑ NatureConnect. Michael J. Cohen's organization, devoted to connecting nature and culture. www.ecopsych.com.

❑ Natural Capital Institute. An organization founded by Paul Hawken to create contacts with a network of organizations devoted to environmental protection and education. www.wiserearth.org.

❑ Project Adventure. A non-profit teaching organization and leader in adventure-based experiential programming since 1971. It provides transformative group experiences and consulting services. 719 Cabot St. Beverly, MA 01915. www.pa.org. Email: info@pa.org.

❑ Playfair. A unique international consulting firm, founded by Matt Weinstein, and devoted to team building and noncompetitive play. See Chapter 7 for an in-depth interview with Matt about his pioneering work and play. Also visit www.Playfair.com. In his TED talk, Matt demonstrates the use of play in recovering from personal loss: https://www.ted.com/talks/matt_weinstein_what_bernie_madoff_couldn_t_steal_from_me.

❑ Playfair's work with prison inmates is featured at: https://www.youtube.com/watch?v=TXwH3SIF9rc.

❑ Play for Peace. An organization whose mission is to use cooperative play to bring together people of communities in conflict. 500 N. Michigan Ave, Suite 600, Chicago, IL 60611. www.playforpeace.org. Email: info@playforpeace.org.

❑ Sharing Nature Worldwide. 14618 Tyler Foote Road box, Nevada City, CA 95959. Joseph Cornell's organization, devoted to sharing nature publications and programs. www.jcornell.org. Email: info@sharingnature.com.

❑ The HUMOR Project, Inc. Founded by Dr. Joel Goodman in 1977, The HUMOR Project is the first organization in the world to focus full-time on the positive power of humor and creativity. Its speakers bureau has presented keynote speeches, seminars, and workshops for schools, hospitals, business corporations, camps, human service agencies, associations, and conventions for more than three million people in all 50 states and on all seven continents. It operates the HUMOResources online bookstore and has sponsored 55 international humor conferences that have featured and honored laughter luminaries like Steve Allen, Sid Caesar, Victor Borge, Jay Leno, Carol Channing, Bob Newhart, Art Buchwald, Gilda Radner, David Hyde Pierce, Lucie Arnaz, the Smothers Brothers, etc. Visit www.HumorProject.com for more on this fun-of-a-kind organization. Email info@HumorProject.com to sign up for their free bi-monthly *Laughing Matters* e-zine that contains humor tips, quotes, cartoons, anecdotes, and the latest in the humor field. The e-zine is designed for anyone who believes in humoristic education and wants to tap the positive power of humor in everyday life and work (put "Humanizing/Humorizing" in the subject line).

❑ The Institute for Earth Education. Steve Van Matre's organization that has been in operation for over 40 years. Offers publications and workshops in the U.S. and abroad. Email: info@ieetree.org.

❑ The Ndakinna Education Center. Founded by Joseph Bruchac, the Center is a nonprofit and charitable organization that offers people of all ages unique hands-on learning experiences; principles of indigenous arts of life; team building; character development; and programs that focus on regional Native American understandings, Adirondack culture, wilderness skills, and awareness of the natural world. www. ndakinnacenter.org.

❑ Training Wheels: A Creative Source for Building Teams. Led by Michelle Cummings, founder, author, and speaker, the organization provides trainings, books, props, and activity ideas. For more info, see www.training-wheels.com.

❑ Wilderness Awareness School (a division of The Awareness Society, a nonprofit corporation). The organization offers programs for youth and adults to promote understanding and appreciation of nature, community, and self through direct experience with wilderness survival skills, tracking, edible plants, and other nature-related topics. www.WildernessAwareness.org.

❑ Wilderness Education Association. The mission of this organization is to promote and support professionalism in outdoor education and its attendant leadership. Establishes standards through curriculum design, implementation, advocacy, and research-driven initiatives. www.weainfo.org.

> *"If you have a garden and a library,*
> *you have everything you need."*
>
> —Marcus Tullius Cicero

ABOUT THE AUTHORS

Dr. Cliff Knapp is a retired professor of education from the faculty of Outdoor Teacher Education at Northern Illinois University (NIU) in DeKalb, Illinois. His teaching career spanned all levels of education, including elementary, junior high, and high school, as well as 29 years of undergraduate and graduate-level instruction at Southern Illinois University (SIU) and NIU.

Cliff was introduced to the field of outdoor education in 1958 when he enrolled in a camping education course at Paterson State Teachers College in Wayne, New Jersey. He continued from there as a camp counselor, director, and co-founder of the Human Relations Youth Adventure Camp in New York's Adirondack Mountains. He received his bachelor's degree in 1961, his master's degree in 1963, and his doctorate in 1973.

Cliff taught science and was the director of resident outdoor education in Ridgewood, New Jersey for seven and one-half years. At several universities he taught courses in outdoor/environmental/place-based education, an undertaking that included curriculum and instruction, teaching methods, science, nature interpretation, environmental ethics, nature arts and crafts, and research.

He has led hundreds of workshops at professional conferences and meetings, such as the Association for Experiential Education, American Camp Association, North American Association for Environmental Education, and the National Wildlife Federation. His workshop topics include Projects WILD and Learning Tree, Leopold Education Project, Children's Nature Literature, Reflecting on Experience, Questioning Strategies, Finding Silence and Solitude, Environmental Ethics, Early Naturalists' Skills, Fire-Making, Native Uses of Bison, and Images of Nature.

Cliff has published widely in the fields of camping, outdoor, and environmental education. He has authored or co-authored 12 books, as well as over 150 book chapters and journal articles. He has written for journals, including *Science and Children*, *Green Teacher*, *Camping Magazine*, *Journal of Experiential Education*, *Nature Study*, and *Taproot*. His latest books include *Lasting Lessons* (1992); *In Accord with Nature* (1999); *Exploring the Power of Solo, Silence, and Solitude* (with Tom Smith) (2005); and *Sourcebook of Experiential Education* (with Tom Smith) (2011). In 2017, he had two companion books (with Joel Goodman) published by Healthy Learning that were adapted and revised from *Humanizing Environmental Education* (1981).

Cliff loves to read, write, teach, carve wooden birds, and walk outdoors. His passion is studying Native American cultures, including participating in sacred ceremonies and collecting indigenous arts and crafts. He teaches and serves on boards of directors for a rural school built in 1883 and a working gristmill first built in 1847. After more than 56 years as an outdoor teacher, he still enjoys sharing what he knows about nature and education. He lives with his wife, Nancy, in Oregon, Illinois. He has three grown daughters, Dawn, Eve, and Jenny.

You can contact Cliff at cknapp@niu.edu.

Dr. Joel Goodman, director of The HUMOR Project in Saratoga Springs, New York, is a popular speaker and workshop leader whose programs on humanistic and experiential education and the positive power of humor and creativity have touched and tickled the lives of millions. In fact, Joel is one of only two professional speakers in the world to have presented in all 50 states and on all seven continents. Since 1968, he has spoken at national and state conferences and at in-house training programs for schools, human service organizations, corporations, non-profits, government agencies, and professional associations.

After receiving his B.A. from the University of Pennsylvania and his M.Ed and Ed.D. from the University of Massachusetts in Amherst, Joel served as the associate director of the Maryland Leadership Workshops and the National Humanistic Education Center. He founded The HUMOR Project in 1977 as the first organization in the world to focus full-time on the positive power of humor and creativity.

Author of hundreds of articles, columns, and magazines, Joel has written/co-authored 10 books, including *Laffirmations: 1,001 Ways to Add Humor to Your Life and Work; Playfair: Everybody's Guide to Noncompetitive Play; Health Education: The Search for Values; Turning Points: New Developments, New Directions in Values Clarification;* and *Magic and the Educated Rabbit.* Joel has also created the unique www.HumorProject.com website and publishes the free *Laughing Matters* e-zine.

Described by New Age magazine as "the first full-time humor educator in the world," Joel's pioneering work has been featured in 7000-plus TV and radio shows, newspapers, and magazines in 175+ countries, including: *The TODAY Show,* PBS, ABC NEWS' prime-time special on *The Mystery of Happiness,* BBC, *Latenight America, Donahue, All Things Considered,* the front page of *The Wall Street Journal, The New York Times Sunday Magazine, The Washington Post, USA Today, Readers' Digest, Successful Meetings,* numerous Associated Press national features, and *The Daily Show with Jon Stewart.*

In 1995, Joel was delighted to join Red Skelton, Willard Scott, and Meadowlark Lemon in receiving the prestigious International Lifetime of Laughter Achievement Award. He is the founder of AHA! (American Humor Association), which includes 165,000 people interested in the positive power of humor. Believing that it is important to "do well and do good" at the same time, The HUMOR Project has provided grants to 500 schools, hospitals, and human service agencies to help them develop services and resources that tap the positive power of humor and creativity.

Joel takes his work seriously and himself lightly, while helping people to get more smileage out of their lives and jobs. His family is most precious to him: wife—Margie, children and their spouses—Adam and Hilda, Alyssa and Jake, and grandson—Jakobe. Joel has participated in sports all his life and loves convening with Mother Nature on his daily long walks with camera in hand.

You can contact Joel at Joel@HumorProject.com.